Teaching, Learning & Psychology

Also available

Professional Studies in the Primary School
Thinking Beyond the Standards
Eve English and Lynn Newton
1-84312-206-5

Professional Values and Practice (Third Edition)
Meeting the Standards
Mike Cole
1-84312-384-3

Teaching, Learning & Psychology

Jane Yeomans & Christopher Arnold

 David Fulton Publishers

David Fulton Publishers Ltd
The Chiswick Centre, 414 Chiswick High Road, London W4 5TF

www.fultonpublishers.co.uk

First published in Great Britain in 2006 by David Fulton Publishers

10 9 8 7 6 5 4 3 2 1

David Fulton Publishers is a division of Granada Learning Limited.

British Library Cataloguing in Publication Data
A catalogue record for this book is available from the British Library.

ISBN: 1 84312 401 7   EAN: 978 1 84312 401 6

Typeset by RefineCatch Limited, Bungay, Suffolk
Printed and bound in Great Britain

Contents

To our parents

About the authors

Jane Yeomans originally trained as a teacher and has worked in both mainstream and special school settings. She is now a Specialist Senior Educational Psychologist for Sandwell Metropolitan Borough Council. She is an Academic and Professional Tutor for the initial training course and the post-qualification doctorate in educational psychology at the University of Birmingham. She is also involved in training teachers and early years practitioners.

Christopher Arnold taught in a range of schools before qualifying in educational psychology. He now works as a Senior Educational Psychologist in Sandwell Metropolitan Borough Council's inclusion support service and is a regular contributor to conferences and publications. He has contributed to initial teacher training and newly qualified teacher induction programmes in the West Midlands for many years.

Preface and acknowledgements

Teaching, Learning and Psychology aims to highlight the important role played by psychology in the processes of teaching and learning. It is aimed, principally, at teachers undergoing training, but we also believe that more experienced teachers would find the text helpful. We have avoided using a title such as 'Psychology for Teachers' as we believe it implies that there is a branch of psychology that only applies to the profession of teaching. The discipline of psychology has a great deal to offer to educators; what we have done is to select some aspects that we feel are most applicable.

Why is there a need for a text such as ours? Many teachers would feel that they are far too busy getting on with the job of teaching to be concerned with any psychological underpinnings for their work. True, teaching is a very pressured job, but we would argue that one aspect of successful teaching is having a secure knowledge base. Psychology can offer this. Knowledge of the psychological theories that underpin essential elements of practice (such as how children learn and develop, how to manage groups, how to monitor and assess) gives you tools to think with. If you know what theory or model underpins your practice, you are in a better position to put things right when problems arise. Otherwise, we would argue that teachers become 'stuck' at the 'tips for teachers' level of practice and are therefore not in a position to problem-solve.

You are bound to work with pupils who have special educational needs during the course of your career. The current climate of promoting inclusion makes it inevitable that pupils who have special educational needs (SEN) will be educated alongside their mainstream peers in their local school. Application of psychology to meeting the needs of this pupil population will be invaluable. Again, psychology offers you tools with which to work in order to determine what is best practice for individual pupils with unique needs. We believe that there is no 'Holy Grail' as far as teaching SEN pupils is concerned.

Unfortunately, it is often implied that there is some kind of different method of teaching for SEN pupils (or subgroups of SEN pupils; the promotion of multi-sensory teaching for pupils labelled as dyslexic is an example) when, in fact, we would argue that effective teaching is effective whether a pupil has SEN or not. In the example cited, we would not argue against multi-sensory teaching; what we would challenge is the assumption that one can label a group of pupils and apply the same pedagogy irrespective of their individual needs. Again, we would argue that knowledge of the psychological underpinnings of pedagogy, or the science of teaching, will enable you to apply models and theories and to know why you are doing so. We hope that the content of this book will help you to do this.

Acknowledgements

Inevitably, the production of a book involves far more individuals than the authors listed on the cover. There are a number of individuals who have supported us in the writing process and we would like to acknowledge their support, as follows:

Pat Evans and Andy Gravenstede, our service managers, for their interest in and support for our writing
Our colleagues Anthony Atwell, Melanie Sutherland and Hardeep Samra for their helpful feedback about Chapter 7
Elaine Ricks, Jackie Charles, Louise O'Connor, under the leadership of Keith Shilton of Cronehills School, for their help with Chapter 5
Helen Merriman for her work in surveying the children in the breakfast clubs
Nick Jarman for his helpful comments
Tracey Alcock, our David Fulton Editor, for her helpful and sometimes challenging feedback
and last, but not least, our families, for being tolerant of our need to spend long periods of time sitting in front of a computer screen.

How to use this book

This book consists of ten free-standing chapters. Although some cross-referencing is made between chapters for the sake of economy, each chapter can be read as a 'stand-alone'. We therefore intend that you should be able to dip into single chapters according to your needs and interests. However, we do recommend that Chapter 1 is essential reading as it introduces the theories that we make reference to throughout the book. We have written subsequent chapters on the assumption that the reader is familiar with the content of this first chapter.

Although there is no progression from one chapter to another, Chapters 2 to 10 fall into two main sections. The first section, comprising Chapters 2 to 5, contain information *about* children and young people: their development, the ways in which they learn and the contexts in which they develop and learn. The second section, comprising Chapters 6 to 10, is mainly *for* children and young people: that is, the chapters deal with the role that teachers play in shaping learning and development. We would recommend that Chapter 6 is essential reading for this section as it deals with effective classroom management. You will find it difficult to implement the strategies and approaches suggested unless you have first established a sound foundation in relation to your classroom management. We would also recommend that the final chapter ('The reflective teacher') is important to read since it will help you to establish some good self-review and -evaluation habits that will assist you in your future professional development.

Throughout the book we have made links between theory and practice, via reflection points and specific activities. It is not essential that you complete all the suggested activities but we have included them as a means of helping you to put psychology into practice on a day-to-day basis. The content of this book will make more difference to your practice if you try things out.

Finally, there are points where we know that we have provided only a minimum of information. These areas have been highlighted by a 'Find out more' box that contains suggestions for follow-up.

CHAPTER 1

Introduction to theories

Introduction and chapter aims

The histories of universal education and psychology are remarkably intertwined. The 1870 Education Act made education compulsory for all. The first university department of psychology in the world was founded in Leipzig in 1879 by Wilhelm Wundt. In England the first department was in Cambridge. Although it was suggested in 1877, the first proposal was rejected on the grounds that it would 'insult religion by putting the soul in a pair of scales'. It was properly established in the first years of the twentieth century. Since then, education has developed and incorporated insights and techniques researched by psychologists. Knowledge of the foundations of psychology is particularly useful in education. If a car goes wrong and needs mending, you can either be shown how to fix the particular problem or develop an understanding of how the car works. The latter will equip you to analyse and diagnose a wide variety of problems, the former will only help with that single situation. Similarly, understanding how people learn will help teachers face a range of situations. Psychology offers such an understanding by providing:

- ways of thinking about and understanding children;
- ways of getting information about children's learning; and
- a vast, world-wide source of information about different people in different circumstances, but collected in a systematic way.

This chapter aims:

- to introduce different psychological theories currently used in education;
- to outline the *ranges of convenience* of the theories; and
- to illustrate how the different theories illuminate different elements of the same situation.

Psychology or psychologies?

Psychology has developed in different directions and there are now distinct *schools* of psychology. Each school has developed different ways of analysing situations and different kinds of explanation. The extent to which a school or theory is applicable is called its *range of convenience*. Each school has a different range of convenience and makes different assumptions about people. Therefore, different schools can draw different conclusions about the same situations. Before embarking on applications of psychology to education, we must understand some of these different schools. This book outlines the following schools:

- biological
- behavioural
- experiential
- social constructionist
- cognitive
- psycho-dynamic.

As we shall see, they all have utility in education.
There are other schools such as:

- Marxist
- feminist
- critical
- post-modern
- emancipatory.

Their omission is simply due to limited space, although there are many valuable insights from these schools of thought, too.

Biological psychology

We are biological beings. We all have bodies with chemical and electrical reactions occurring within them. The biological school looks at the workings of our bodies within the social contexts in which they are found. Behaviour, thoughts and feelings are understood in the context of our physical make-up. Developmental psychology is an example of biological psychology and studies the ways in which we change as we grow. It looks for universals in development in children's lives.
Consider the following sequence:

1 grasping

2 holding

3 making marks on a surface

4 scribbling

5 copying

6 writing.

This represents the stages leading up to writing and illustrates a developmental sequence. Such sequences of stages have the following characteristics:

- Each stage has a particular focus or repertoire of behaviours.
- The behaviours at each stage are different from those in other stages.
- Children go through each stage in the same order.

Stage theories of development have been criticised as lacking evidence. However, recent developments in mathematics have revived interest. It is now possible to produce simple mathematical models that account for the ways in which one stage of stability arises from another. Piaget's stage theory is considered in Chapter 2.

Links between psychology and biology

Evidence of the relationship between psychology and biology can be found in research on heart attacks and personality types. Friedman and Rosenman (1974) analysed behavioural habits and the likelihood of suffering from heart disease. They concluded that there were two different approaches to stressful situations and that one was more likely to lead to heart attacks than the other. Type A characteristics involved individuals becoming impatient and angry when confronted by stressful situations; type B individuals tended to be able to relax and not become agitated. Type A behaviours include:

- having difficulty sitting still;
- needing to win competitive games;
- thinking of doing more than one thing at a time;
- becoming anxious when needing to wait for something;
- needing to be on time; and
- getting impatient with others, believing that they can do the task faster.

Type B behaviours include:

- being able to sit and relax;
- stopping to appreciate a good view;
- remaining calm in frustrating circumstances;

- being patient with others; and
- lacking a sense of urgency.

There are many other features. Fortunately, it has proved possible to teach type A individuals to respond more like type B with a positive impact on health.

Biological ideas can extend further into behaviour. Charles Darwin described the process of natural selection and the survival of the fittest organism leading to the evolution of the species. Richard Dawkins has refined those ideas to consider genes mutating, with those that offer survival advantages being selected. The fittest genes are passed on. If genes influence behaviour then some behaviours, too, might be passed on from one generation to another. We can consider the 'survival of the fittest behaviours'. This is called *sociobiology*.

A controversial illustration of this can be found in the work of Buss *et al.* (1992). They investigated sexual jealousy in men and women by asking subjects to imagine their partners either having sexual intercourse or establishing a relationship with someone else. Physiological reactions were measured by looking at heart rate and skin conductivity (arousal causes sweat, which changes electrical conductivity). The reactions were different. Eighty-five per cent of women showed more anxiety imagining the relationship than the intercourse, while 60 per cent of men became more anxious imagining the intercourse rather than relationship. This is consistent with the predictions made by the sociobiological theory. Men cannot be absolutely certain that children carry their genes, whereas, until very recently, women could be. It is in the woman's interest to secure a partner who will provide for them and their child, so a relationship with another is more threatening than intercourse. It is in the man's interest to ensure that the partner does not carry any other man's genes, so the intercourse is more threatening than a relationship.

Our final illustration of biological models examines individual differences in drug and alcohol addiction. The development of residential accommodation in tower blocks in the 1960s led to large numbers of young mothers being housed in areas away from their previous communities. Many found themselves powerless and lonely and became depressed. They went to their doctors who prescribed an anti-depressant drug, Valium. This led to addiction to the drug. Do we consider the addiction to be biological in origin or an adaption to an unsatisfying environment? Cox and Klinger (1988) demonstrated differences in susceptibility of rats' brains to alcohol. It is possible to breed rats selectively to increase susceptibility to alcohol. This points to a genetic link. So is addiction to alcohol a result of a genetic difference in the brains of alcoholics? Should we consider alcoholism a disease? Cox and Klinger's model suggests that people weigh up the advantages and disadvantages before deciding to drink. Alcohol might bring about a better mental state than not drinking. Use of alcohol may be an adaption to a social situation rather than a disease.

Critical periods

Developmental psychology considers evidence for critical periods in development. This needs some explanation. If some experiences are not available at certain points, does lasting and irreversible damage occur? Evidence for this was provided by examination of 102 persistent offenders, aged between 15 and 18, by John Bowlby for the World Health Organisation in 1951. He concluded that the offenders demonstrated anxieties which dated back to unsatisfactory relationships in early childhood. The young people had been separated from or rejected by their mothers in early life. Many had been raised in children's homes. He concluded that absence of a secure bond with a caring adult caused serious and long-lasting damage. His work was used to change the ways in which young children in hospitals were treated. Nurses were encouraged to give 'tender loving care' to children. Although Bowlby's work was criticised for highlighting only one factor in an extremely complex field, his ideas led to a wide acceptance of the need for young children to have stable adults in their lives. An application of Bowlby's work (nurture groups) is described in Chapter 2.

The concept of critical periods has also been applied to children's academic learning, in the context of neurological bases for educational programmes. This application of the concept is discussed in Chapter 4 in the section about the role of the brain.

What constitutes an explanation?

The nature of the insights and explanations of learning generated from a biological perspective tends to fall into one of two categories:

- *Causal* explanations look at the biochemical processes around behaviour. The suggestion that some brains are different and more susceptible to alcohol is one example of this.
- *Functional* explanations look at how the behaviour (or belief or feeling) serves the organism. The work by Buss on sexual jealousy is such an example.

Within this school, learning is considered to be a process of *adaption* to the environment. Biological analyses are good at discovering predispositions to learning and behaviour. These may include physiological responses such as anger and love, ways in which children interact in school and addictive behaviours. They are not particularly useful in examining *how* we learn skills and behaviours. For this we turn to *behavioural* psychology.

Behavioural psychology

The professor of psychology at Harvard in the 1890s was William James (brother of the author Henry James). In his textbook of psychology he asserted that:

'Psychology is to be treated as a natural science'. He proceeded to separate psychology from philosophy and rejected introspection in favour of observation. He made three assumptions to create this type of psychology:

- Mental events could be examined with the same discipline as a physicist treated his/her research interest.

- 'Mental facts cannot be properly studied apart from the physical environment of which they take cognizance' (James 1905). In other words, the environment in which the learning occurs needed to be considered as a factor influencing the learning. When a person learns something, they must be able to demonstrate what has been learned in a form external to the human body. So they must be able to *do* something different to prove that they have learned it. It is not enough for a child to *say* that he/she has learned their lesson, they have to act differently next time.

- Complex behaviours are combinations of simpler ones. Behaviour can be analysed by dividing into parts.

- Principles of learning can be found in other species. We can understand our own learning by studying learning in rats, pigeons, chickens etc.

What constitutes the environment needs elaborating. Certainly the context or setting in which the learning occurs is a part, but so is the history of events following the learned act. Let us illustrate this with two celebrated studies.

The work of Ivan Pavlov

The name Pavlov is associated with dogs salivating to bells. Actually, he was interested in digestion and developed a way of measuring saliva production in animals. To his surprise, he found that, after a while, the animals would begin to salivate *before* the food arrived. They would start when they heard the experimenter arrive. They associated the experimenter with the food. Pavlov investigated this and found that if a bell was sounded just before the presentation of the food, the dog would salivate. Furthermore, the dog would continue to salivate even if the food was not presented. If the pairing of the bell and the food was removed, the dog would eventually learn not to salivate to the bell.

This study gave rise to the concepts of *stimulus* and *response*.

The food was an *unconditioned stimulus*. The saliva was an *unconditioned response*. The bell was a *conditioned* stimulus. The saliva produced by the bell was a *conditioned* response.

This process has become known as *classical conditioning*. Its application in human learning is great. If a child has been frightened by a particular event in a particular place, the place may evoke fear, even though the frightening feature is not present. The conditioned responses tend to be biological in nature: fear, pleasure, panic and laughter. Even heart rate can be classically conditioned. We can be taught to relax to a particular piece of music or art. Classical conditioning highlights the role of events *before* the observed behaviour.

The work of B.F. Skinner

The importance of events *after* the behaviour can be illustrated by the work of the psychologist, Skinner. He summarised the work of others by suggesting that rewards and sanctions are important stimuli to learning. If an action is followed by a reward the action is more likely to be repeated. If an action is followed by a sanction the action is less likely to be repeated. What constitutes a reward or a sanction is simply defined. If an event is likely to result in the action being repeated it is a considered to be a reward. If it is likely to result in the action not being repeated it is considered to be a sanction.

Many of Skinner's studies were with rats in boxes, with a bar which was linked to a device giving sugar pellets. The arrangements by which the rats got the small sugar pellets were changeable, but the vital element was the examination of the events *after* the behaviour. This is known as *operant* conditioning. Arguably, we work for our salaries (or likelihood of future earnings). This is an example of operant conditioning. A user of a gambling machine uses it in the *hope* of a reward. As we will see later, there are many different ways of arranging action and consequence in schools.

If we combine classical and operant conditioning we begin to see the relationship between the nature of the environment and behaviour. We need to consider *both* the setting and the history of the consequences. This framework is sometimes described:

Antecedants	Behaviour	Consequences
A	B	C

This approach is called an *Applied Behaviour Analysis*.

REFLECTION POINT AND APPLICATION ACTIVITY

Antecedents and consequences

Take a moment to consider some problematic aspect of the behaviour of a child that you know. What are the antecedents to the behaviour and what are the consequences? If you wanted that child to behave in some different way, how could you change the antecedents or the consequences?

Challenges to classical and operant conditioning

So far, learning can be seen as *adaption* to the environment. Classical conditioning highlights the role of the context, and operant conditioning highlights the history of the consequences. However, learning can depend on other factors. The social psychologist Albert Bandura is associated with social learning theory. Consider the following study.

Imagine nursery children viewing an adult behaving aggressively towards a doll. The children are left with the doll. What did they do? They copied the adult and were aggressive towards the doll. The experiment went further in measuring total aggressive responses in the children (not just towards the dolls). The children who had watched the aggressive adult showed more aggression overall. The experimenters varied the ways the children were shown the aggression. Some saw live models, others saw a film and a third group were shown cartoons. For comparison, some were shown non-aggressive models and a control group did not see any model behaviour, but were just given the dolls. Children shown live, filmed and cartoons of aggressive acts were between four and eight times more likely to act aggressively towards the doll than children who did not see a model. Those who saw a non-aggressive model were less likely to act aggressively towards the doll than those who did not see a model.

We have to conclude that the children learned the aggressive responses from simply watching the adults. Remember that there were no rewards or corrections used; nor was there any history of using that context for aggressive purposes; the children were learning vicariously, through observation. Bandura called that process *modelling*.

Modelling can be used theraputically. A successful treatment for snake phobia uses this method. The subject is invited to imitate someone who undertakes increasingly fearful activities with the snake. The subject is guided in touching the snake with a gloved hand then touching it without gloves and eventually letting it crawl over them. The technique is called 'live modelling with participation'.

The extent to which a model will be imitated is dependent on a number of factors:

- the skills required – these may include physical, social or intellectual;
- the perception of the situation – if the situation is seen as threatening, the response may be different from seeing it as challenging;
- expectations – what might happen if you behave in that way;
- subjective values – what the relative gains and losses are likely to be; and
- is it achievable? Can you make a plan to do this?

The nature of the model is a variable. If the model is perceived positively then the behaviour is more likely to be copied.

Learning in this school of psychology is through children's experience of the consequences of behaviour in given contexts. If a child cannot *do* something different at the end of a teaching cycle, then no learning can be said to have taken place. Behavioural psychology has a vast contribution to make to understanding and promoting children's education; it provides a clear rationale for the banning of corporal punishment in school. If adults hit people to resolve difficulties, children are likely to copy. It clarifies the roles of school. It is not enough simply to create a context and reward and correct children's learning; the adults in the school must act in ways similar to those they expect from the children. Exposure to violent TV and computer games is not likely to promote positive behaviour. Even cartoons are influential on young children.

We also find here the *economic* view of people. In transactions we weigh up the advantages and disadvantages of a particular course of action. If we think that we will gain more than we will lose, we act; if not, we will avoid. The items being gained and lost may not be tangible. A person may appear to act selflessly, yet believe that their standing in other people's eyes may go up. For children in school, the admiration of peers may make the misbehaviour worthwhile, whatever the subsequent sanction from the teacher.

Behavioural psychology is not good at investigating what people *think*. For that we must turn to *experiential* psychology.

Experiential psychology

This is also known as *humanistic* psychology and starts from the premise that we all have unique and individual experiences of life. Therefore, we can all behave, believe and feel differently from each other. A meaningful enquiry does not seek to find universal laws of learning, but allows each to tell its own story. We are able to reflect on our own actions and intentions. The use of this type of psychology is to increase the individual's sense of well-being through self-awareness and autonomy.

The link between autonomy and well-being was illustrated in a study of care homes for the elderly. Homes that were run without the residents' involvement led to signs of depression and helplessness. Homes that involved residents in decision-making led to happier residents who lived longer. However, total autonomy can be a frightening thing. Believing that you are totally in control of yourself can lead you to believe that no-one can tell you what to do or offer help and guidance. It means taking *responsibility* and being *accountable* for your actions. Fear of freedom leads to defences being built. It may be easier to delegate responsibility to some external group, such as 'society' or a moral/religious code.

Questions significant for this school include the search for meaning and empathy.

CASE STUDY

A school was concerned about a 13-year-old boy who had a reputation for getting into trouble. At the beginning of the new school year he was quiet and well behaved. The school was pleased, but after about three weeks his behaviour became very disturbed. He was close to being excluded. The school asked the educational psychologist to investigate. He convened a meeting with the school's special needs co-ordinator and the child's mother. He asked about the events leading up to that point. While the SENCO talked about the child's behaviour, the mother remained silent. She barely made eye contact. The psychologist asked the mother if anything had changed in the life of the boy in the last month or two. Tears began to fall from the mother's eyes. 'Yes,' she said, his dad packed his bags and left in the middle of the summer holidays.' The boy was particularly close to his father and went on trips in his lorry. What was so painful was the reaction from her own mother. She was being blamed because she did not try to stop the father from leaving. She did the ironing while he was packing his bags. 'HOW COULD YOU?' the grandmother had screamed. The fact was that she was so distressed she needed the routine of ironing. 'How did the boy react?' asked the psychologist. 'He went to his room and laid out his school uniform on the bed.' The mother was becoming more composed. The SENCO then gently told the mother about her own experience of being left by her husband. She had gone to work that evening to take a Year 9 parents' evening. The truth was that she needed the routine to help her cope with the shock. The psychologist suggested that children in this situation tend to take their distress to those people they trust rather than those they dislike.

The interview served to create a shared understanding about the child's behaviour and generate some empathy for the child and his mother. This enabled the school staff to see the boy in a different way. His behaviour was not 'bad', but a reflection of his distress. The outcome was better for all parties.

The issue of personal choice is found here. We can exercise choice if we are aware of alternatives and have a sense of autonomy. It is through self-awareness that we gain insight into ourselves. However, there are cultural and individual differences that affect this. While one role of religion can be seen as filling a need for meaning, there is little evidence that people who are not religious are more concerned about these issues than others. A sense of religious meaning can lead to acts of terrorism or of tremendous kindness and compassion. The task of experiential psychology is to help people understand each other and free individuals through self-knowledge.

Learning in this school is personal and individual. Applications to teaching and schools are found in the areas of examining the relevance (or meaning) of the curriculum and creating shared understandings of the lives and experiences of people in schools. They focus on individuals. However for tools and approaches to groups we must turn to the *social contructionist* school of psychology.

Social constructionist psychology

Have you ever found yourself behaving in an unusual way? Do we act in different ways in different contexts? Do children behave and use the same language in the street, in a classroom and with their parents? For most of us we accept that we are influenced by the social context in which we are placed. We might consider that our very *identities* are different in different contexts. To help understand these processes we must understand *selfhood*.

We can accept that a person has a self-contained mind, unique to that individual. We all have a sense of 'I'. 'I' am the person writing this chapter. 'I' have thoughts and cause actions. However, if I stop and reflect, I can create an image of 'me'. Clearly, I cannot see 'me' as others do, but I have experienced myself as a person through other people's eyes. I can separate the 'I' from the 'me'. The image that I have of myself has been created from my interactions with other people. I can glimpse myself through the eyes of those people. If a child is brought up being told that they are 'good', the child will see themselves as good. If, however, the child is constantly being told how bad they are, they will see themselves as bad. If we lived in just one social group, we might have only one sense of self. However, we find ourselves in many different settings. I am a husband, parent, friend, psychologist, son, manager, colleague, customer – the list could go on. In each setting I have a slightly different image of myself. This extends to the way I might behave and the kind of language I might use. We could say that my selfhood is *distributed* across the different contexts. If someone wanted to know me, they would need to study me in each of these different contexts.

THEORY AND PRACTICE LINK

New situations and sense of selfhood

Have you ever found yourself in a completely new context in which you did not know the social rules and you made some kind of social mistake? You may have misinterpreted an instruction. What did you do and how did you feel? How do you think the others viewed you? How did you try to restore your sense of selfhood?

Understanding the role of context is important when viewing children in school. The similarity of school with home varies considerably. For some children the social rules of school will be very different from those of home. Children will need different amounts of direction when they start school. If a child has constructed a 'self' from being told that they are bad, they may attempt to confirm that view of themselves by behaving badly in school. Teachers may praise children for good work and behaviour only to find that an individual proceeds to spoil the work or behave very badly. We think of some children as being unable to take praise or positive feedback. One way of understanding this is by considering the child's self-image. If the child sees themselves as bad, being told that they are good conflicts with their self-image. This internal conflict needs resolving. It is difficult to hold conflicting thoughts at the same time. One resolution is to demonstrate to the adult that they are, actually, wrong. The child is bad, the work is rubbish and the child will show this by misbehaviour or destroying the work. For the adult it would be tempting to confirm that view of the child by agreeing that they are bad. If they did so, the child would continue with the negative self-image. If, however, we aim to help the child see themselves in a more positive light we can work on the child's view of themselves *in school* as being positive. We have to accept that learning is context-bound.

When building a 'self', the role of language needs to be examined. Knowledge is not 'out there' waiting to be discovered, but generated between people using language. We cannot assume that the same word has the same meaning for different people even if they speak the same language. At a simple level, the words 'bad' and 'wicked' have very different meanings according to the context in which they are used. A high court judge may describe a person as 'wicked', meaning that they have broken a legal or moral code, whereas a teenager may use the term to mean fantastic or wonderful.

We can illustrate this point by examining the terms used to describe the range of inherited conditions in children in the first half of the twentieth century: 'Mentally defective, incorrigible, feeble-minded, dull, backward, imbecile, mentally weak, idiot, degenerate, congenital criminal' (Burt 1927). These were all acceptable descriptions of children.

We can consider shared assumptions about education. Teachers tend to have been successful in schools as pupils. Many teachers come from families with relatives who work in education. Education has been seen as a career offering positive opportunities for the future. There are tacit assumptions that school is useful and that, although it may not all be enjoyable, it is in the pupil's interest to work hard and comply with the requests of teachers. Many other children, however, may come from families which do not share this view of school. The experiences of these family members may not have been positive, and children may not trust teachers to hold their best interests. Such pupils may be less inclined to comply with directions from teachers.

Learning in this school is social. Knowledge and understanding of the world occur through interactions between people. This psychology has many far-reaching applications in schools. It creates an understanding of the differences in behaviour that children display in different contexts and offers a way of teaching children to see themselves in more positive lights, raising self-esteem and promoting well-being. It requires the language used in classes to be checked for shared understanding. It enables the attributions that teachers make of causes of children's actions to be examined. It emphasises the role of social groups in shaping our thoughts, feelings and behaviours. It does not seek to examine the individual's mental processes involved in learning. For this we must turn to *cognitive* psychology.

Cognitive psychology

The term 'cognitive' comes from the Latin word for knowledge. The basic assumptions of this school might be familiar to many and possibly represent conventional views of what psychology is and what psychologists do. The processes of acquiring knowledge are analysed in terms of:

- Perception – visual, auditory, tactile, taste and smell
- Memory – the ability to recall events and actions (see Chapter 4)
- Information processing – how the brain uses sensory information (see Chapter 4)
- Attention – how we select what we attend to
- Motivation – why we do things (see Chapter 5)
- Concept development – how we build our knowledge of the world (see Chapter 4).

There are others, but we will concentrate on these as they illuminate educative processes in schools. We will illustrate some of these with one application, although the researched applications are vast in number.

Perception

The term *perception* refers to the way we organise and respond to information gained through our senses. We learn how to interpret this information. For example, in relation to our perception of sound, there is evidence that we *learn* how to do this by adapting to our acoustic environments. Best and Avery (1999) studied perception of clicks by Zulu and English speakers. In English a click is not part of our spoken language, but in Zulu it is. Best and Avery studied the sensitivity to clicks of each side of the brains of Zulu and English speakers. They found that English speakers were equally sensitive to clicks when presented in either ear, whereas the Zulu speakers were more sensitised to clicks presented in the right ear than in the left. The right-ear signals are processed by the left-hand side of the brain, which is associated with speech processing.

In English we can see the role of context in auditory perception by considering the following experiment. Warren (1970) produced tapes of the following (the * represents a cough inserted in the tape):

- It was found that the *eel was on the axle.
- It was found that the *eel was on the shoe.
- It was found that the *eel was on the table.

Subjects were asked what they heard. They restored the missing sound, but exactly which sound depended on the context.

Similar studies can be found for the remaining senses. For example, see Blakemore and Cooper's studies of visual perception in kittens. This can be found in Arnold and Yeoman's (2005) *Psychology for Teaching Assistants*.

Information processing

Cognitive Behaviour Therapy (CBT) is an example of a practical application of the information processing element of cognitive psychology. In this model problems are dealt with by helping clients to understand the mental processes underlying their difficulties. For example, anyone who has experienced a panic attack will be able to relate to the terror that the racing heart and loss of breath creates. Sufferers often believe that they are having a heart attack and are about to die. Recent work suggests that the individuals are responding to a change in their body's state. They interpret the change as being threatening and respond to the perceived threat by becoming more anxious and by producing adrenaline. This, in turn, increases the heart rate. So the individual's heart rate increases because of the beliefs that the person holds. The techniques of CBT are beyond the scope of this text, but one technique involves looking for *thought mistakes*. The individual is asked to examine what they thought was happening (I thought I was dying) compared with what actually happened (I had a panic attack). The success rate for this kind of therapy is impressive.

Attention

The information received by our senses is vast. Our minds may organise it along useful lines, but the extent to which we can respond to information is limited. We attend to information which we find meaningful. A simple experiment serves to remind us that we do not respond, simply, to particular senses. Dichotic listening describes a task in which subjects wear headphones which give different signals in each ear. Subjects are asked to concentrate on the signal coming in one ear and repeat what is being said. If the subjects are listening to a story and the signals are reversed (so the left ear signal is suddenly fed to the right, and vice versa) the subjects will continue repeating the story rather than the signal from the requested ear. Attention appears to be a finite commodity in these circumstances.

Experimental investigations into attention have suggested attentional *filters*. Information is filtered out if it is considered irrelevant. We learn to attend to our names, so when a teacher suspects that a child is not attending, the introduction of their name may regain their attention. In our visual fields we attend to the information found in the centre, but novel features in our peripheral vision will attract our attention. So we may be concentrating on reading a book or watching TV, but someone entering the room quietly will be noticed.

Children are described as having *attention spans*. The descriptions tend to suggest inherent qualities in children. Like memory, this omits an important variable – the environment. A child may attend to a new cartoon, film or computer game for hours at a time, yet not concentrate on learning new letter sounds for more than a minute. Can we suggest that the child has a limited attention span? It is more meaningful to describe the child's response to different tasks in different environments.

Explanatory fictions

Unfortunately, our enthusiasm for analysing mental processes can lead us down blind alleys. When we look at a child who is not remembering his/her letter sounds we may say that 'they have a poor memory'. What is the evidence that they have a poor memory? They are not remembering their letter sounds. The hypothesis does not provide us with additional information, yet places the explanation for the lack of learning with hypothesised mental processes inside the child's head.

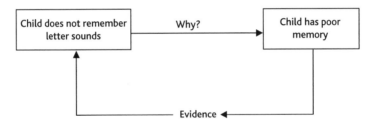

Figure 1.1   The explanatory fiction

The same cycles can be made for inattention (or short attention span) and lack of motivation. Such explanatory fictions neither offer new information nor suggest ways of helping the child. They can, however, provide justifications for not teaching children effectively.

Psychodynamic psychology

The best-known name in psychology is probably Sigmund Freud. He founded an approach in the nineteenth century that is still in widespread use today. He developed a view of mankind that he considered universal. His theory has a number of fundamental assumptions:

- In addition to mental processes of which we are aware, there exist mental processes of which we are unaware. These are called *unconscious* processes.
- Our behaviour and thoughts are influenced by primitive *drives* and *motives* which are found in the *unconscious* parts of our minds. Therefore we are not always aware of the real goals of our thoughts and actions.

- Asking people about their thoughts, feelings and actions will not always give you a full picture as they are unaware of these unconscious processes.

- A powerful aim of our unconscious mind is to protect us from anxiety. We develop *defence mechanisms* to do this. These mechanisms may appear irrational, and might include transference, denial, projection, splitting, displacement, introjection and rationalisation.

- Early childhood experiences are important determinants of our future interactions with the world. Early relationships can set lifelong patterns of perception, action and feelings.

To illustrate the first point, consider a young child (say four years old) who has been told not to eat the raspberries in the garden. The child does eat some and goes indoors, where a parent sees raspberry remains around the child's mouth. The parent asks the child if they have eaten some. The child lies and says 'no'. The parent says, 'I think you have'. The child is baffled. How does the adult know? We have no difficulty understanding the behaviour of the child, although the child is unaware of how the parent knows.

If we look at adults who behave in unusual ways we can attribute motives to which they may not agree. A teacher who is always volunteering for additional duties may be considered ambitious, yet may hotly deny it ('I'm only doing it for the kids').

Ideas from psychodynamic psychology have found their way into everyday life. The concepts of *being in denial, inferiority complex* and *sex drive* arose from this school (although not necessarily from Freud; the inferiority complex was described by Alfred Adler). When commentators suggest that the attacks on Iraq in 2003 were influenced by a powerful country's *anger* at being attacked in 2001, they are using psychodynamic concepts. When people act in irrational ways the psychodynamic psychologist seeks explanations from unconscious processes. If the subject of the explanation suggests alternative accounts, the subject may be *denying* the process.

Within this school of thought there are two themes – the *development* of defence mechanisms and *insight* into them. We are able to understand ourselves and overcome the influences of our unconscious minds through increasing self-knowledge. Although this may come though extensive psychotherapy, it can arise through insights found through careful reflection.

Evidence and psychodynamic psychology

The psychodynamic school has many sides. It provides a theory of the structure of human minds, it creates a basis for helping people through therapy and it contains cross-cultural information. For example, the psychodynamic view is that desire for incest is universal and societies have created taboos and have repressed these feelings. Elements of this idea are testable, as recent studies of the *Westermarck Effect* can illustrate.

Westermarck was a Finnish sociologist who noticed that early childhood inter-actions and proximity (e.g. children playing together) reduced the likelihood of sexual interest later. This was recognised as a mechanism that reduced within-family sexual contact (sibling incest). Studies in the 1970s suggested that the genetic disadvantages associated with breeding within families were enough to account for a genetic bias away from such practices. However, there may be a gender asymmetry. The cost of incestuous mating may be higher for women than for men. A study of chimpanzees by Pusey (1980) found that female chimpanzees emigrate from their natal groups to find mating opportunities from unrelated males, thus maximising the survival of their genes into future generations. Not all societies, however, display female dispersal. In species where the male disperses, this arises from the breeding opportunities being taken by a few dominant males. In other words young, less dominant males need to disperse to find breeding opportunities at all, thus strongly suggesting a socio-biological account of the Westermarck Effect.

There is certainly a tension between the socio-biological and psychodynamic schools of psychology which both aim to cover similar human behaviours. How-ever, the strength of psychodynamic work is such that practitioners are likely to continue for many decades to come.

Applications

These schools of psychology can be applied to people in different ways. Within education these include:

- individuals – pupils, parents and teachers etc.;
- groups – classes, families, staffrooms, managers etc.; and
- institutions – schools, local education authorities, government offices, inspection services etc.

THEORY AND PRACTICE LINK

Applying models of psychology to a case study

The following is based on a real case.

Billy (not his real name) is 14 years old. He has attended his local secondary school in an urban area which is defined as socially deprived by all statistical measures. His behaviour in school has become very difficult. He regularly responds to teachers setting him tasks by burying his head in his hands and telling the teachers to f*** off. The school's discipline code is implemented and he is told to leave the class. If this happens more than three times he is sent home, and if that does not result in improved behaviour, he is excluded from school. This has just happened and the school, reluctantly, is carrying out the exclusion. Billy was abandoned by his mother and left to fend for himself at the age of twelve. Neighbours notified Social Services who found him alone in his house with no food and no adults to care for him. He was looked after and fostered by a local lady who had raised her own children. She lives in the same area as his previous house and seems extremely fond of him. She is determined to stand by him whatever the difficulties.

He never knew his birth father, but his mother had relationships with a number of partners. She used drugs and drank alcohol during the day. She would appear at the gate of the junior school in an apparently drunken state. When asked, she said that Billy was rude and abusive at home. She said that she had seen a TV programme on hyperactivity and had asked the doctor for some tablets, but the doctor had refused. Overall, Billy's health is good, although he is inclined to steal food. His educational attainments are very weak. His reading is similar to that of six-year-olds and he finds it difficult to write, unless it is copying. However, he gets bored copying. He draws very well and seems to enjoy it. While he has been suspended from school he has been mixing with some older excluded pupils in the area. There are suspicions that he may be in contact with groups involved with breaking and entering houses. This is not confirmed.

The school has been subject to 'special measures' until very recently. The acting head teacher is unsure whether the permanent job will be his. Some staff feel unsupported in a very difficult area of town. Morale is low. Although some staff feel very sorry for Billy, he is seen by many as a waste of time and they think that the school is better off without him.

Different elements of Billy's plight are highlighted by different schools of psychology. Consider the case and analyse the key elements.

Question: What are the different ways forward for Billy based on the different psychological perspectives? Are some mutually exclusive?

Summary

It is our intention to present a view of psychology as offering a range of different perspectives and approaches. While some of these approaches may find greater or lesser utility when applied to particular human problems, there is an element of personal preference on the part of the psychologist or teacher. Psychology cannot offer one single definitive view about questions such as 'What is learning?', as what constitutes learning may differ according to the favoured orientation of the person concerned. A behavioural view would be that learning requires the person to be able to do something new, while an experientialist view would concentrate on the *sense* of having learned something as a result of a new experience. Thus there is no single way to approach human problems; each may have a contribution to make. What unifies the discipline, however, is the common ethical code. Psychology must have the best interests of the individual at heart. Whether the psychologist concentrates on analysing actions and behaviours, or thoughts and dreams, the welfare of the client is paramount. In conclusion, this chapter has:

- outlined a range of psychological theories;
- discussed the utility of different theories; and
- suggested initial applications in education.

CHAPTER 2

Child development

Introduction and chapter aims

Human beings have the longest period of development and maturation until adulthood is reached. Childhood is recognised as a distinct aspect of human development and has led to a number of systems and disciplines that focus specifically on this stage of human development. The discipline of developmental psychology studies age-related changes that take place in a variety of areas of human development. The types of areas of study are physical, linguistic, social, emotional, intellectual, moral and spiritual development.

Creation of an education system is recognition that children are not fully formed and mature individuals and that some degree of formal education is thought to be beneficial in helping them to reach adulthood. It is interesting to note, however, that education for all children is a comparatively recent development in Great Britain. Until 1970, some children were labelled as 'ineducable' and did not have access to schooling. They were cared for in junior training centres. This pupil population comprised children with multiple, complex and profound disabilities.

We have assumed that child development will be covered in some depth in your training, so this chapter will only give an overview. It's aim, therefore, is as follows:

● to look at the contribution that psychology makes to our understanding of child development and the implications for teaching.

Child development: nature or nurture?

How do we develop into the person that we are? How much of our individuality is shaped by our genetic and biological inheritance, and how much is shaped by external influences, such as the way we were brought up by our parents? We often refer to these questions as being part of the nature/nurture debate. The answers to these questions are not just the province of psychology; philosophy had debated these questions long before psychology emerged as a specific discipline. The ancient Greek philosophers Plato and Aristotle held differing views on this subject; Plato thought that all knowledge was inherited, while Aristotle thought that experience played a part. In the eighteenth-century Enlightenment movement, these opposite views were held by John Locke and Jean-Jacques Rousseau. Locke viewed children as a *tabula rasa* on which experience made its mark, and there was nothing inherited that would shape the individual. In contrast, Rousseau argued that children are born with inherent traits (he thought that children were inherently good) and needed protecting from the evils of society.

More recently, in the twenty-first century, advances in technology have contributed to our knowledge and understanding of our biological heritage. For example, the human genome project has identified all the genes in our DNA (there are between 20,000 and 25,000 genes). Genes associated with specific diseases have been identified. The project is moving on to investigate the interaction between genes and the environment in relation to the study of disease. Our understanding of the structure and function of the brain is another contribution to understanding our biological heritage. For example, some mental health problems are associated with abnormal brain chemistry (schizophrenia is associated with high levels of dopamine and depression with low levels of serotonin). Abnormal functions of areas of the brain have been linked with abnormal behaviour; for example, the function of the amygdala in the brain is linked with personality disorder, since this part of the brain deals with emotions.

Environmental influences on development

Given the advances of technology, it is tempting to think that we will soon be able to explain away all of our individuality on the basis of biology. It would be dangerous, however, to ignore the effect of the environment; evidence for the effects of the environment on development can be found. Physical characteristics can be affected by environmental factors; for example, there is strong evidence to support the link between low birth weight and maternal smoking. The amount and type of nutrition children receive will affect height and weight. Perhaps more controversially, there are many claims that diet and nutrition play a part in children's behaviour and on their adjustment.

The example of physical characteristics being affected by environmental factors is a fairly straightforward cause-and-effect link. Other aspects of environmental influences on development are not as straightforward. The terms 'disadvantage' and 'deprivation' are common currency in education. These terms imply some causal link between a family's social and economic circumstances and the child's development. As a consequence, children's attainments and progress in school are adversely affected. Successive governments have sought to tackle the effects of disadvantage and deprivation. In the 1970s, Educational Priority Areas were set up in four areas of the UK (Liverpool, Birmingham, Yorkshire and south-east

London). These areas were given additional resources from central government to enable them to offer compensatory education programmes. The idea of community schools was promoted in the 1970s, where the emphasis was on 'cradle to grave' education. The work of Eric Midwinter (for example, Midwinter 1972) was instrumental in the promotion of these forms of compensatory education. With more than a little sense of *déjà vu*, the mid-1990s onwards has seen the introduction of Education Action Zones, where the formation of partnerships between schools, local education authorities and community organisations in areas of disadvantage is designed to raise standards via good education and lifelong learning. SureStart is an initiative introduced to disadvantaged areas which aims to achieve better outcomes for children, parents and communities. Finally, the Extended Schools initiative aims to make links between the school and community and to create community learning centres. The Government Green paper *Every Child Matters* (DfES 2003) sets out far-reaching plans for providing 'joined up' service delivery to families experiencing disadvantage and includes plans for the further development of initiatives such as SureStart and Extended Schools. Although the initiatives are new and different, the underlying philosophy that it is possible to compensate for disadvantage is not really that different from that of the 1960s and 1970s.

Clearly, a great deal of central government educational policy is driven by tacit agreement that the environment impacts on development and consequently on schooling. As teachers are a crucial aspect of the education system, you cannot afford to ignore this relationship.

The dangers of over-emphasis in the nature–nurture debate

There is no easy answer to the question about the relative impact of nature and nurture. There are dangers inherent in over-emphasising one or the other when we consider the causes of children's developmental difficulties. An example of such over-emphasis is given below.

In 1943, Leo Kanner described the characteristics of a group of children with whom he had worked. These children had no language, little desire to communicate, and showed obsessional behaviour and resistance to changes in routine. In 1944, Hans Asperger (independently of Kanner) described the characteristics of children very similar to those described by Kanner, except that Asperger's children had some language and functioned higher intellectually. These groups of children are what we would today call 'autistic' or on the 'autistic spectrum'. After Kanner and Asperger had made their observations, Bruno Bettelheim conducted a study of children displaying these characteristics. Bettelheim concluded that these children were the subject of social and emotional deprivation, caused by inappropriate parenting. He used the term 'refrigerator mothers' (a descriptor first used by Kanner) to describe what he proposed was the type of cold and unfeeling parenting that led to children being autistic. His views are described in his book *The Empty Fortress* (Bettelheim 1967). Bettelheim's view became accepted as the cause of autism, and as a result autistic children were treated as if they had a mental illness. Autism was seen as a form of childhood schizophrenia. This view of the cause-and-effect link between parenting and autism was subsequently demolished, following many studies of autistic children and their families. The focus shifted to seeing autism as a developmental disorder, possibly neurological in origin. Imagine the distress experienced by families labelled as 'cold' or 'unemotional', who saw their children being treated as mentally ill.

In summary, we have seen that, increasingly, medical science is able to provide more and more knowledge about our biological heritage, but that the environment continues to play a part. As professionals it could be dangerous to accord too much importance to one or the other, since our knowledge of both is partial. Changes in our knowledge base can have a profound influence on the way in which we view development that is different from the norm. On balance, the stance that the environment affects development is probably a more optimistic view, since it can then be argued that schools and teachers should be able to make a difference. If we take the view that biological or genetic factors are the most important aspects of development and difficulties, then we might just begin to think that we can exert little influence over our pupils.

Psychological perspectives of child development

Chapter 1 looked at a number of schools of psychology and showed how the theories of each of them might influence the way in which children's difficulties are construed. The same is true of child development. The way in which psychologists view child development will vary according to the theories that underpin their thinking. Consequently, views of atypical development will also vary.

Why should this matter to teachers? You could take a pragmatic view that the theory doesn't matter, you simply deal with difficulties or problems as they are presented to you. The very fact that you are reading this book probably means that you want to have a deeper understanding of your role, and in particular how psychological theories can shape your ideas about teaching and learning. Your view of child development will affect the way in which you deal with children on a day-to-day basis. The process of making explicit a number of views about child development will help you to reflect on your views and to perhaps identify the influences on your thinking. Also, you might wish to promote one particular theory or view having read this section.

This section will look at four different psychological perspectives on child development: cognitive; sociocultural; psychoanalytic; and behavioural.

The cognitive perspective of child development

Cognitive psychologists are interested in inner mental processes. In terms of child development, this means that a cognitive perspective would focus on the development of the intellect.

Jean Piaget's theory of intellectual development

Jean Piaget's theories are probably the best known in relation to children's intellectual development. Piaget was originally a biologist but became interested in psychology after meeting Freud and Binet (Binet developed intelligence tests; you will meet him in a later chapter) and after having three children of his own. He developed his ideas about intellectual development by observing his own children and by conducting a series of experiments with children that involved mental processes.

Piaget suggested that intellectual development passed through a number of stages and that these stages were age-related.

Table 2.1   Piaget's Stages of Development

Stage	Age	Description
Sensori-motor	Birth to two years	The child makes sense of the world using its senses and movement. An example might be a baby putting objects in its mouth in order to explore them.
Pre-operational	Two to seven years	As language develops, the child gradually uses symbols to represent objects. An example at this stage is the emergence of pretend play.
Concrete operations	Seven to eleven years	The child begins to think logically but needs concrete situations and examples in order to do so. An example of this stage could be children needing to use their fingers in order to add totals.
Formal operations	Age 12 onwards	Abstract thought is apparent, without the need for concrete objects or examples. Hypothetical thought emerges. An example of this stage would be taking part in a debate about good and evil.

Piaget's theories contributed to significant changes in thinking about Primary Education from the late 1960s onwards. The Plowden Report, published in 1967, advocated a developmentally appropriate curriculum and recommended a major shift away from a teacher-led curriculum to a child-centred one. The concept of readiness was emphasised, based on Piaget's ages and stages view of children's intellectual development. This concept led to major changes in teaching. For example, in the teaching of reading, 'readiness' skills such as shape discrimination or auditory discrimination were taught before the child was exposed to books or print in any formal teaching context.

Piaget's views about intellectual development were challenged by the work of Margaret Donaldson (1978). She felt that Piaget had underestimated children's abilities. She argued that children's responses during tests or experiments might be influenced by what they think the adult wants them to say or do. Donaldson repeated many of Piaget's experiments, but used materials that were familiar to children. For example, her investigation of conservation of number involved 'naughty teddy' who came along and muddled up some sweets. She also rejected the rigidity of Piaget's 'ages and stages' view. Instead, she suggested that children use different modes of thought but that they do not discard one mode in favour of the next, more developmentally sophisticated, mode.

Jerome Bruner's theory of intellectual development

One other cognitive approach to intellectual development is that of Jerome Bruner (for example, Bruner 1960). Bruner, like Piaget, suggested that there were stages of intellectual development, but in contrast to Piaget, he did not link these to particular ages. Bruner suggested that intellectual development went through three stages, as follows:

- the *enactive* stage, where the emphasis is on doing, using actions and objects;
- the *iconic* stage, where pictures are used; and
- the *symbolic* stage, where abstract thinking is used.

Therefore, the sequence in Bruner's model is:

concrete $\Longrightarrow$ pictorial $\Longrightarrow$ symbolic

Intellectual development: summary

This section has looked at the development of intellectual skills. Although Piaget's work was carried out many years ago, his influence on education has been profound. Today we might not take such a rigid view of the development of intellectual skills, but if we think about our teaching we are probably using his theories. For example, if you teach Key Stage 2 children, you probably use concrete objects or examples in your teaching. Think about the use of apparatus in maths. In key stages 3 and 4 you probably rely less on concrete examples and use more debate and discussion in your teaching. We assume that children in secondary education have reached a level of thinking that permits abstract thought.

The following is designed to help you to think about some of the issues surrounding child-centred education and a developmentally appropriate curriculum arising from Piaget's theories.

REFLECTION POINT AND APPLICATION ACTIVITY

Intellectual development

In 1967, the Plowden Report said: 'At the heart of the educational process lies the child'.

In 1981, the Department for Education and Science said: 'The school curriculum is at the heart of education'.

Which view do you think prevails today? Why?

How would the two views influence the way you teach? Are they mutually exclusive?

Is it possible to be child-centred but with the curriculum taking centre stage?

Activity

Choose a lesson plan. Identify which of Piaget's stages your plan mainly focuses on. Do the ages and stages correspond?

Now plan a lesson that incorporates enactive, iconic and symbolic stages.

The socio-cultural perspective of child development

At the beginning of this chapter we considered the relative impacts of nature and nurture on the developing child. It was suggested that neither could, or should, be ignored. Environmental influences were seen to be a major feature of a behavioural perspective on child development, to the extent that this perspective would pay little regard to heritability.

Another perspective that is environmentally influenced is the socio-cultural perspective. In this perspective, the role of culture and cultural development is emphasised. In this perspective, therefore, development is shaped by the child's culture. Here we see an attempt to integrate psychology and anthropology (the study of human cultures).

The socio-cultural perspective was developed by psychologists in the former Soviet Union. Soviet psychology considered western individualistic emphases in psychology as being 'bourgeois'. The collective view of humanity, as reflected in both political thought and the organisation of society, were major themes in Soviet psychology. Pavlov was the most revered psychologist. His behaviourally orientated work fitted with a view that the human organism could be modified and that human behaviour had a strong physiological component.

The work of Lev Vygotsky

Lev Vygotsky was one of the main proponents of a socio-cultural perspective. His goal was to develop Marxist psychology. Marxism emphasises the role of history, because we can understand a society or culture by looking at historical events that have shaped it. Although it is possible to see the Soviet influences in Vygotsky's work, his work was suppressed by Stalin due to his interest in paedology, or the study of the child. This interest involved attention to individual differences including the measurement and assessment of these differences, which Stalin regarded as anti-Soviet. (It has also been pointed out that a contributory factor might have been the fact that Stalin's son failed some of the educational tests that were routinely administered in schools.) Stalin banned the practice of psychology in schools and Vygotsky's work was not known in the West until the latter part of the twentieth century (Vygotsky died young in 1934).

Although Vygotsky was a proponent of paedology, his major contribution to psychology is his work about the interaction between culture and development. Vygotsky thought that development was attributable in part to growth and maturation but that psychological functions were culturally mediated (mediation is a particular way of learning, where the learner does not interact directly with stimuli, but instead has these stimuli filtered and interpreted) (Vygotsky 1929). Development takes place in a cultural context at a macro (societal) and micro (family environment) level. These cultural influences shape the way in which the child thinks and processes information. In a socio-cultural perspective, tools and artefacts are used to reflect and shape culture. Therefore, individuals do not interact directly with their environment but are mediated via use of tools and artefacts. Language is an example of a mediational tool. In a Vygotskian perspective, cognition is developed via social interaction. Adults use language to transmit culture which, in turn, shapes the child's cognition. This notion of transmission leads to the concept of the *zone of proximal development* (ZPD). The ZPD is the difference between the child's assisted and unassisted performance.

The socio-cultural perspective: implications for teaching

A socio-cultural perspective helps us to understand development in a cultural context. There are potential difficulties where home and school cultures differ. Before we make judgements about children's development, we should try to understand the culture that has shaped that development. In addition, children's cultural development can be promoted in schools via a culturally appropriate curriculum. Music and history are two subjects where a range of cultures might be affirmed.

Social interaction and language as the basis for the development of cognition can be reflected in classroom practice. How much teacher talk is directive and how much is genuinely discursive? A Vygotskyan perspective would emphasis the role of discourse in the classroom. The notion of the ZPD should influence the way in which we assess and then work with children. We should not only assess the actual level of a child's development but also their assisted level of development. If we do this, we can identify the next steps of learning.

THEORY AND PRACTICE LINK

Comparing Piaget and Vygotsky

Piaget thought that development led learning.

Vygotsky thought that learning led development.

What do you think?

Think about the way in which your pupils learn and how you structure your teaching.

Are you influenced by the developmental stage you think your pupils have reached, or are you influenced by the learning you think needs to take place?

APPLICATION ACTIVITY

Cultural development

If you teach key stages 1 or 2, choose a subject area. If you teach key stages 3 or 4, carry out this application activity with reference to the subject you teach.

What cultures are represented in your school's pupil population?

Make a list of culturally relevant activities that you could incorporate into the subject you have chosen as your focus, or the subject that you mainly teach in school.

If you are still in initial training, do this application activity with reference to a teaching practice placement.

The psychoanalytic perspective of child development

The psychoanalytic perspective traces its origins back to Sigmund Freud and relates principally to social and emotional development. This perspective takes the view that there is a relationship between personality and childhood experiences. Therefore, adult mental health problems are attributed to childhood traumas. Freud viewed childhood development as a series of stages that were related to sexuality (Freud 1905). Therefore, a 'Freudian' view of atypical development would revolve around traumas at one of the stages of development. Freud's stages of development were oral, anal and genital.

The work of Eric Erikson

Eric Erikson came from the psychoanalytic tradition. He also viewed development in stages, but emphasised social aspects of development. He suggested eight stages of development that covered the entire human lifespan (Erikson 1950). Erikson called each stage a 'crisis'. In order for development to progress, the crisis at each stage had to be resolved. Social or emotional development difficulties were attributed to unsuccessful crisis resolution. Erikson's stages are shown in Table 2.2.

Table 2.2   Erikson's Stages of Development

Stage	Description
Trust versus mistrust: neonate to age 1	The child is dependent on adults for all aspects of physical and emotional care. If needs are met then attachments are formed; if not, then mistrusts develops.
Autonomy versus doubt: ages 1 to 2	The child gains increasing control over his/her body. Confidence and independence develop. The child has to cope with choice. Positive approval from carers is important. Doubt arises if carers are disapproving or over-protective.
Initiative versus guilt: ages 2 to 6	The child is curious and adventurous. Responsible behaviour is beginning to be learned, so the child gradually restrains impulsivity. Boundaries are important but should not be enforced in such a way that the child feels guilty or ashamed if their behaviour isn't acceptable.
Competence versus inferiority: ages 6 to 12	The child makes the transition from home to school and begins to have his/her intellectual needs met. A sense of competence develops.
Identity versus role confusion: ages 12 to 18	This is the period of adolescence, where a typical question is 'Who am I?' At this stage, resolution of earlier conflicts is integrated so that the young person is able to deal with the crisis of identity that arises during this period.
Intimacy versus isolation: ages 19 to 40	Relationships are important. At this stage commitment to a relationship commonly emerges.
Generativity versus stagnation: ages 40 to 65	At this stage, the individual has children and creates the next generation.
Integrity versus despair: ages 65 to death	This is the stage for reflecting on life. Is it fulfilled or unfulfilled? Has life been a success or disappointment? Fear of death is reduced by positive outcomes at this stage.

Theories of attachment

The psychoanalytic approach to child development also uses theories about *attachment* in order to explain reasons for atypical or poor social and emotional development from early childhood onwards.

John Bowlby's theory about the effects of separation is a significant contribution to ideas about attachment and subsequent social and emotional development. (Bowlby 1951). The World Health Organisation asked Bowlby to look into this issue of separation. He studied young people labelled at the time as 'juvenile delinquents'. Seventeen of a sample of 44 delinquents had experienced some kind of separation before the age of five. Bowlby made a link between attachment and the development of social conscience. He suggested that the relationship between a mother and her child was quantitatively different from any other kind of relationship, and drew on ideas about imprinting from studies of animals. Although Bowlby's theory is more than fifty years old, his influence can still be seen in the development of nurture groups (Boxall 2003). The idea of a nurture group was developed by Marion Boxall in the 1960s. Nurture groups are based on the notion that social and emotional difficulties may be attributed to inadequate nurture at an early age. Therefore, the experiences offered in a nurture group aim to offer the nurture that children have missed. A nurture group operates in a separate room in school and has enhanced staffing levels. Adults model positive relationships. The set-up and layout of the room reflect a home environment, with a dining table and comfortable chairs. Children are not placed in a nurture group full-time, so inclusion in their mainstream class remains a feature of the intervention.

The psychoanalytic perspective: summary and application exercise

A psychoanalytic approach to child development focuses on the effect of early childhood experiences on later development and uses these early experiences as an explanation for atypical development. The following gives you an opportunity to think about this approach and, if you have access, to investigate nurture groups in a little more detail.

THEORY AND PRACTICE LINKS

Nurture groups

The purpose of this activity is to help you to look at the way in which theory is reflected in practice. In order to do this you will need access to a nurture group and will need permission to observe the group and talk to the adult in charge.

Spend some time observing the group and list the activities that you see. How does each activity link to nurture and help to form attachments?

Look at the adults in the group. List the things that they say and do. How do these contribute to forming attachments and positive relationships?

If it is appropriate, talk to the children. What do they say about the group? Why do they think they are in the group?

Talk to the adult in charge. Ask about the principles that the group is based on. What does the adult understand about attachment theory and how it is translated into practice in a nurture group?

REFLECTION POINT

How would a theory of attachment influence the way in which you would treat a pupil with social and emotional problems?

How would a psychoanalytic view of child development influence the way you interact with the children in your class? What assumptions would you make about any difficulties they presented?

The behavioural perspective of child development

The behavioural perspective gives very firm emphasis to the influence of the environment, thus taking the 'nurture' view in the nature–nurture debate, often to the complete exclusion of any contribution of 'nature' to development. Therefore, development can be shaped by parents, teachers and the wider community. A behavioural perspective does not take an 'ages and stages' view of child development; rather, it is an underlying theory that seeks to show how development of specific skills is the result of the interaction of the child with his or her environment.

Language development as an example of the behavioural perspective

The principles of classical and operant conditioning have already been introduced in Chapter 1. Here we need to consider how these theories, and the behavioural perspective generally, will influence views about child development. Language development will be used as an example of a behavioural approach to an aspect of child development. The behavioural view of language is based on that of B.F. Skinner, who put forward his theory of language development in his book *Verbal Behavior* (Skinner 1957).

A purely developmental approach to language development generally takes an 'ages and stages' view. The acquisition of language is linked to the emergence of specific skills at particular ages. There is an accepted sequence in which skills emerge, so that even where development is slow, it still follows the same sequence. The broad sequences of development for expression and understanding are shown below:

Table 2.3 Stages in language development

	Expression	Understanding
0 to 6 months	Crying: develops different types of cry. Vocal sounds begin to emerge.	Responds to caregivers' voices.
6 to 12 months	Range of vocal sounds expands – laugh, squeal, cry – and are used in different contexts. Babbles: gradually imitating speech intonation. Single words might be apparent by 12 months. Lots of imitation.	Recognises different tones of voice. Responds to simple, routine instructions (such as 'wave bye bye'). Responds to name.
12 to 18 months	Vocabulary of single words expands rapidly. Begins to put two or more words together ('all gone'; 'need a wee'). Continues to imitate.	Understands longer instructions and single words. Understands 'no'.
18 months to 2 years	Vocabulary expansion continues. Begins to use complete sentences but with sometimes incorrectly applied rules of grammar ('I goed to the shop'). Speech production may be unclear.	Understands questions.
2 to 3 years	Continued vocabulary expansion. Asks questions. Speaks in longer sentences, begins to use more than one sentence at a time. Still some unclear speech.	Understands longer and more complex instructions. Understands questions that use 'who' and 'where'.
3 to 4 years	Can talk about a past event using several sentences in a sequence. Vocabulary continues to grow.	Understands a range of words that relate to concepts such as time.
4 to 5 years	Growing ability to sustain a conversation through several turns and to maintain the topic. Most sentences are grammatically correct.	Understands a wider range of words related to concepts such as time, space, distance, quantity. Understands more complex multi-part instructions ('find your coat and your hat').

In contrast, a behavioural theory of language does not link skills with ages, but shows how language develops as an interaction between the child and the environment. According to Skinner, language is a behaviour; therefore, we speak as a consequence of the environment that we are in. Language is gradually built up from simple to complex, so the behavioural perspective does contain some notion of a hierarchy or sequence in development.

A behavioural perspective stresses the use of specific techniques. These techniques can be applied to language development. The following gives examples of applications of behavioural techniques to language.

Table 2.4 Behavioural approaches to language acquistion

Technique	Description	Application
Reinforcement	A response to behaviour. The type of reinforcement will determine the likelihood of the behaviour being repeated. Positive reinforcement increases the chance of behaviour being repeated.	Child says 'pop'. Dad gives the child a drink.
Shaping	The desired behaviour is modified gradually, by accepting successively close approximations to the target behaviour.	Target language is 'Please may I have some pop?' The child's language is shaped through successive approximations: 'Pop please', 'Want pop please', 'Please have pop', 'Please may I have some pop'.
Prompting	Assistance so that child can demonstrate target behaviour. Prompts can be physical, gestural or verbal.	Child says 'pop'. Dad prompts for use of 'please' by saying: 'What's the magic word?' Child recognises this as a prompt to use the word 'please' and says 'pop please'.
Fading	A gradual removal of prompts given to the child to ensure that the child is not dependent on prompts to produce correct target behaviour.	Dad fades the prompt by waiting for child to say please, rather than giving the full verbal prompt.

Skinner argued that operant conditioning could be applied to language. The notion that behaviour is reinforced by its consequences in a language context is simply that we receive a response to our language that is a natural consequence. So we are given what we ask for, our question is answered, we receive a reply to our comment or observation, and so on. Skinner analysed language into a number of functional units. He made up labels for these units, such as a mand (derived from de*mand*), which is used to request, or tact (derived from con*tact*), which is used to label or comment. Skinner also emphasised the importance of imitation in language acquisition, using the term *echoic repertoire*.

An application of the behavioural approach to language development

The behavioural perspective has declined in popularity in education (although a great many programmes aimed at increasing appropriate behaviour are based on behavioural principles, as will be discussed in detail in Chapter 6). However, an approach to teaching language and communication skills that is very popular in special education is based on behavioural principles. This approach is the Picture Exchange Communication System, or PECS (Frost and Bondy 1994). This is a type of augmented communication, that is, it uses means other than spoken language in order to teach language and communication skills. The basic idea of PECS is that the child uses a picture symbol as a substitute for a word. The first stage of PECS is where the child exchanges a picture for a highly desired item (often this is food). Here we can see the application of behavioural principles. Access to a desired item is contingent upon offering the picture (*reinforcement*). At the very early stages, *prompting* is used. The child can be physically prompted to offer the card, but this level of prompting is *faded* gradually. Communicative behaviour is *shaped* through a series of stages:

- Stage I: a picture is exchanged for one desired item.
- Stage II: the child travels to find a picture and to take it to an adult.
- Stage III: the child selects a picture of the desired item from a group of pictures (discrimination).
- Stage IV: the child uses 'I want . . .' sentences.
- Stage V: the child respond to the question 'What do you want?'
- Stage VI: the child uses pictures to comment about aspects of his/her environment.

PECS is an application of a behavioural approach that would not generally be found in mainstream schools. However, with inclusion of pupils with increasingly complex special educational needs in mainstream settings, it is possible that you might come across this system. It is an intervention often used with children diagnosed with autistic spectrum disorder (ASD). ASD children experience significant difficulties with language and communication and PECS has been successful in encouraging such children to communicate purposefully.

The behavioural perspective of child development: summary and application activity

This section has shown how behavioural principles can be applied to language development, in general terms and in a specific application used with children who experience significant impairment to their language and communication development.

Summary

Knowledge of child development is an important part of the background knowledge of teachers. This chapter has shown some very differing views of child development. These differences arise from the various schools of psychology that are covered in this book. It is important that you reflect on these different perspectives as they will influence the way in which you take account of developmental issues in your teaching. In particular, the different psychological perspectives will have a bearing on views of atypical development. The application activity that concludes this chapter will help you to apply some of the different theories about child development in the context of a pupil experiencing problems in school.

APPLICATION ACTIVITY

Here is a brief 'pen portrait' of a child experiencing some problems in school:

Susan is 12 years old and has just started secondary school. She's having a tough time. She hasn't made many friends and she often doesn't help herself in this respect as she can appear to be rude to both teachers and peers. This has landed her in trouble on several occasions and the head of year has put her on report. She is a mixed-heritage child and there aren't many other mixed-heritage children in school. The white and black children call her names so she doesn't feel that she fits in anywhere. Susan also finds lessons difficult. She often doesn't understand what teachers are talking about and wishes that she was back in Year 6 because her teacher would always explain things again to her and use concrete examples to help her to understand. She misses the Caribbean cookery club that was run at her primary school because most of her friends were there.

Things at home aren't good either. Susan is the eldest of five children and her mum doesn't seem to have time for her. Often she's asked to look after the little ones. Her mum has suffered from mental health problems and she was often not around when Susan was little because she was in and out of hospital being treated. Susan was looked after by a succession of relatives.

Teachers should take account of a number of aspects of development. What would each perspective of child development have to say about Susan's difficulties? How would these views lead to intervention in order to make school a much happier place for Susan?

CHAPTER 3

Teacher perceptions of children

Introduction and chapter aims

Schools are essentially social places in which children and adults interact. There are numerous factors underpinning the types of interaction they have. Education is probably unique in employing previous consumers of a service to deliver the next generation of services. Teachers have been pupils and bring memories and experiences to their work. It is inevitable that we have our own concepts of learning and create ideas about the children we teach. In this chapter we will consider evidence that:

- teachers develop theories about children;
- these theories are subject to factors which can lead to unreliable conclusions;
- these theories have an impact on educational outcomes for children; and
- changing theories about children can change the educational outcomes for those children.

The halo effect

In 1920, the psychologist Thorndyke wrote *A Constant Error in Psychological Ratings*. He outlined evidence that we develop overall impressions of people and use them in estimates of other attributes. If, for example, we gain an impression of a person as strong on certain dimensions we tend to estimate them as high on others. We call this 'the halo effect'. Conversely, if we estimate someone as weak on one attribute, we may apply this to others. This is known as the 'Devil effect'.

Thorndyke's work looked at army officers. If they were asked to rate their men in terms of intelligence, physique, character and leadership, there was a strong cross-correlation. Soldiers rated highly on one dimension tended to be rated highly on the others.

More recently, the issue of school uniform has been debated. Posner (1996) looked at the issue of school uniform and school discipline. Schools tend to produce favourable data. Children in uniform are better behaved and the schools they attend have less vandalism and fighting. However, there is no significant body of evidence to support this. When more systematic studies are conducted, the connections are not made. The *perceptions* of better behaviour and reduced violence may be caused by the halo effect. The theory that children who comply with uniform may also comply with behaviour is implicit for some teachers. It can work the other way round too. As late as the 1960s some schools encouraged teachers to wear academic gowns. Some did and some did not. Children assumed that those who did not were less well qualified than those who did. However, some well-qualified staff chose not to wear gowns. In fact, these generally younger staff tended to be more popular because they chose not to comply with the uniform expectation.

What function does the halo effect have? One hypothesis is that it reduces anxiety for the perceiver. If our experience of developing concepts leads us to link certain attributes, to consider each case from scratch is cognitively expensive. It requires less processing to link this case with previous ones. Biologically, there may be more survival value in responding quickly to new stimuli than assessing each attribute anew. 'Shoot first and ask questions later' may derive from a much more primitive response to hostility than the expression itself.

Evidence in education – teachers' perceptions

When teachers mark tests, do they demonstrate bias consistent with the halo effect? An American study looked at a maths test with five items for each child. They were asked to score each of the five elements of a performance-based test. The study was looking at the effect of training on the nature of the scoring. Those teachers who had received training from an experienced director were more accurate than self-trained raters, but there was no difference in halo effect. An untrained group demonstrated significant halo effects. Children with the same performance were more likely to be rated higher if they had higher scores on other elements.

In a study of children's behaviour, Stevens *et al.* (1998) showed teachers video tapes for two groups of children, one 'normal' and the other having diagnoses of attention deficit hyperactivity disorder (ADHD) or oppositional defiance disorder (ODD). Children who displayed more opposition were assessed more hyperactive and less attentive. The observation of opposition to the teacher affected the ratings of attention and hyperactivity. This suggests a negative halo related to opposition. Other studies have explored this. Walker (1987) looked at the differences between teacher and parent descriptions of children thought to exhibit ADHD. The teachers reported a boy–girl ratio of 7 : 1, the parents of the same children reported a ratio of 3 : 2. The writers suggested that gender was less likely to be a feature of parental reports, but far more a factor for teachers. Jackson and King (2004) used video tapes of children portraying ADHD and ODD and asked teachers to estimate the degree of disturbance for a variety of behaviours. They found that there was a significant halo effect for ratings of oppositional behaviour and hyperactivity. Pupils were rated higher on scales for one factor because of the presence of the other. Teachers who saw a child display opposition were more likely to give a higher rating for hyperactivity and children who displayed hyperactivity were more likely to be given higher oppositional ratings. Of particular interest was the difference in ratings of boys and girls. The boys' portrayal of opposition generated significantly higher ratings of hyperactivity than those of the girls. Given that children can be allocated a drug regime on the basis of teacher and parent reports alone, the study offers some important reasons to pause for thought.

Evidence in education – parents' perceptions

The beliefs of parents and their influence on educational outcomes for children have long been researched. We will examine a recent study which looked at the relationships between:

- parents' level of education;
- parents' implicit theories about child development;
- children's cognitions concerning self; and
- academic performance.

The study was undertaken in Turkey (Hortaçsu 1995). The parents' theories of child development were categorised into either *perspective* or *categorical*. The former consider that child development is influenced by a large number of different factors interacting together. Development occurs within a dynamic system of multiple influences. Categorical theories, however, reflect beliefs in single causes as determinants of development. These can be heredity or environment and tend to be embedded in single situations rather than the possibility of different developmental contexts. In Turkey, the categorical parental beliefs tend to be associated with strict disciplinarian parental styles and the need for children to obey, while the perspective parental beliefs are associated with more responsive and child-sensitive parenting styles. The researchers found that the distinction in belief was more marked in fathers than mothers. Additionally, there was a link between educational level and belief. Parents with higher educational attainments and qualifications tended to have more perspective theories, while those with fewer educational attainments held more categorical theories about child development.

Children's cognitions about themselves were elicited by statements designed to look for beliefs about external control as opposed to self-efficacy. Examples of statements reflecting each are:

External control
Powerful others: If I have a bad teacher, I won't do well in school. If I want to be an important member of the class, I have to get the popular kids to like me.

Unknown control
When I do well in school, I can't figure out why. When another kid doesn't like me, I don't know why.

Self-efficacy
Internal control: If I get bad grades, it's my fault. If somebody likes me, it is usually because of the way I treat him/her.

Social efficacy
You have to carry some things home after school; asking another kid to help you is good for you. Some kids need more people to be on their team; asking to be on a team is good for you.

The findings were:

- Higher levels of mothers' education led to perspective beliefs and rejection of categorical beliefs. This resulted in higher levels of attainment in their children, lower insecurity and lower perception of external control.
- Higher categorical beliefs, however, resulted in decreased child efficacy and lower educational attainment.
- Fathers with categorical beliefs fostered insecurity in children.
- Fathers with perspective beliefs fostered child perceptions of self-efficacy and higher educational attainments in children.

The researcher concluded that there was a significant link between parental beliefs about child development and the educational outcomes for children. The link, however, was not simply between educational attainment of the parents and their children, but was mediated by the different belief systems. The research did not consider the possibility of changing the beliefs of the parents to influence the outcomes for the children, so the suggestion of a *causal* link is not proven.

Changing perceptions – Rosenthal and Jacobson's study

So far we have illustrated the link between beliefs, perceptions and outcomes. There are many other studies in this field, but the question so far undiscussed is the impact of *changing* perceptions of teachers. The most complete study of this has become a landmark in educational research. In spite of never being replicated by other researchers (it would be difficult to do, as we shall see) there are sufficient studies supporting the halo effect to support its overall findings nearly forty years later. The study has become known as 'Pygmalion in the Classroom', by Rosenthal and Jacobson.

Background to study

Their starting point was the 'self-fulfilling prophesy' and Rosenthal and Jacobson cited several examples. As far back as 1900 a study considered the events surrounding a government bureau which had installed a new counting machine. This required the operators to learn new skills (rather like modern typing). The operators were expected to produce 550 cards per day. They soon achieved this, but some attempted to beat this score. They became tense and stressed to the extent that the management instructed the operators not to exceed this amount of work. However, later the department took on an extra 200 workers. They knew nothing about the limit nor the operation of the machine, but within three days they were producing 700 cards per day and went on to produce three times that amount per day with no ill effects. The first group of workers demonstrated the self-fulfilling prophecy; the second, who were unaware of the prophecy, were not limited by it.

Much closer to the Rosenthal and Jacobson study was one by Bavelas (1965) which considered the influence of expectation on perception of performance. Employees were given tests of intelligence and manual dexterity. Supervisors were asked to evaluate the job performance of the employees. The researchers told the supervisors that certain employees had done very well in the tests. The supervisors reported more favourable evaluations for these people. However, the researchers had randomised the scores. This would simply be another example of the halo effect, but an additional element was found. The employees whose supervisors were told had scored well actually *increased* their work output in line with the expectations. This suggests that the halo effect can influence the subject as well as the observer. These studies provided the background for Rosenthal and Jacobson's research.

Rosenthal and Jacobson's experiment

Rosenthal and Jacobson took a school in the USA located in an inner-city area with an ethnically mixed population. The profile is worth examination as it has parallels with some inner-city areas in the UK. One child in six came from a Mexican heritage. Within this group the language competence in Spanish varied from fluent to very little. The group tended to stick together at school. There were 30 per cent transfers per year. So the school population was never stable. Children were moved out by parents when a place at the 'better' school nearby became available. The majority of the families had fathers who were unskilled or semi-skilled and extreme poverty was a feature of the area. The attainments of the children were among the lowest of the 12 schools in the area. The other schools with poor attainment also catered for children from similar socio-economic and ethnic backgrounds.

The school operated a streaming system. Each school year had three classes: fast, medium and slow. Allocation to group was by attainment, mainly in reading. The assessment of attainment was conducted by the teachers over the year. Although teachers could recommend a change of group allocation, this was rare. Teachers were required, however, to recommend allocation of pupils to groups at the end of each academic year.

The allocation of the children to the different groups was uneven:

Mexican children in the school	17%
Mexican children in the fast group	6%
Mexican children in the slow group	29%

The Mexican boys and girls were distributed evenly, but this was not the case for the non-Mexican children:

Non-Mexican boys in the school	53%
Non-Mexican boys in fast group	38%
Non-Mexican boys in slow group	69%

So non-Mexican boys tended to be allocated to the slow group.

The study sought to vary the expectations that the teachers had of the children. This was done by the administration of a new test, the *Harvard Test of Inflected Acquisition*. The test was actually a standardised general ability test, but the staff were told that it was based on variations of rates of children's learning. Children's learning showed spurts and plateaux over time. The test uncovered children who were due to have a learning spurt.[1] The teachers were told that they were assisting in the standardisation of the new test and administered the test in May 1964, January 1965 and May 1965. They were not told of a further follow-up test to be conducted in May 1966. The test looked like a conventional test used in schools at the time. There were verbal and non-verbal elements. The test was marked by researchers, not the teachers.

The teachers were informed of about 20 per cent of each class who were due to have such a spurt. Assignment to the group was random. The research considered the influence of:

- age (or grade)
- track (slow, medium or fast)
- gender
- ethnic or minority group.

[1] In fact Van Geert (1994) has provided a convincing account of non-linear cognitive development. These ideas were explored for reading acquisition by Arnold (2002).

The results deserve careful consideration. They have been subject to mis-reporting through repeated telling, like 'Chinese Whispers'.

Results

Age of pupil

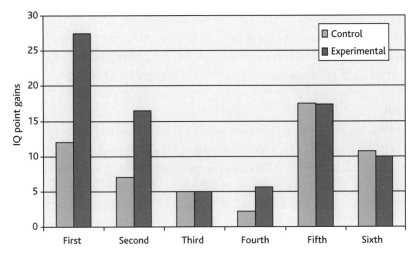

Figure 3.1   IQ gains by grade

These results were subjected to statistical analysis. The chances of obtaining this pattern by chance are less than one in fifty. The results for the first and second grades are particularly striking and were analysed further.

Furthermore, the experimental group had greater gains in all IQ bands. All of the differences were statistically significant. They were highly unlikely to have arisen by chance. We must remember that the allocation to group was random. The only variable was teacher expectation.

Type of gain

The test that was applied measured *verbal* and *non-verbal* skills separately. The research looked at gender differences in both grades 1 and 2 compared with 3 to 6. Only the gains for the experimental group in grades 1–2 are statistically significant. There were no statistically significant differences for grades 3–6.

The results for *non-verbal reasoning* showed differences in gains for grades 1–2 and those for 3–6 were close to being statistically different. When the results were combined to look at all six years, they became highly statistically significant. The research looked for differences between track (or stream). They were not found. These advantages were the same across high, medium and slow tracks. There were, however, differences by gender and type of reasoning. Boys gained on verbal tests while girls gained on non-verbal tests.

Ethnicity of pupil

Finally, for this study, we shall present the results from the minority group of children from Mexican-heritage families.

The results overall suggested that these children were slightly more advantaged by favourable expectations than the other children, but the results could have been from chance. However, the team developed a 'Mexican-ness' index for the children's faces and correlated the gains with facial characteristics. The results were positive for boys, but not for girls. Boys with more Mexican faces were more likely to gain from being in the experimental group than boys with less Mexican faces. It must be stated at this point that the numbers were quite small.

Durability

The results so far seem to support a hypothesis that teacher expectation was influential with years 1 and 2, but not with older children. Recall that the children were tested after two years. These results can be thought of as reflecting durability of findings. We will present these findings in the same format as used above (Figure 3.2).

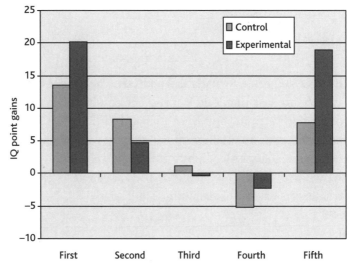

Figure 3.2 IQ gains by grade – two years later

Note that the actual grades were one more, as the children were a year older. The same identifier is used for simplicity. Only the differences in the fifth grade were statistically significant. Even the apparent advantages for the first-grade group could have occurred by chance. The authors describe the advances by the older children as 'a baffling question'.

The dramatic gains in first and second grades were not found to persist, but separating the verbal and non-verbal IQ found the advantages for girls overall – boys' verbal and girls' non-verbal were statistically significant.

The Mexican-ness question was re-examined and boys who looked more Mexican tended to show greater advantages than those who looked less Mexican, but the numbers were extremely small and so the results should be treated with caution.

Replication

While the reported study has received wide readership, the replication is less well known. Indeed, many experienced educational researchers believe that the study has never been replicated.

Rosenthal and Jacobson did run a quasi-replication in a school 3,000 miles from the first school. There were significant differences between the schools. The new school had children from predominantly middle- and upper-class families. The teachers were given the names of the 'special' children after a term of contact. The results were compared with those from the fast track in the first school as these provided the nearest group when comparing attainment.

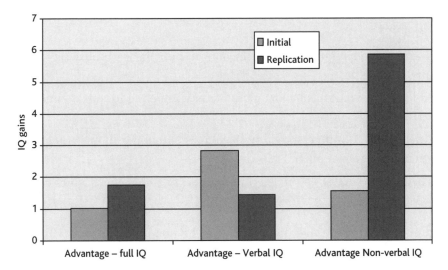

Figure 3.3 IQ gains for both schools

The differences in non-verbal advantages were statistically significant.

Durability
The children were re-tested after three semesters. By now they were with teachers who were not aware of their 'special' status. The results from the replication were similar to those from the fast-track group in the first study.

The patterns between the two groups were also similar.

Summary of findings

In summary, the studies carried out by Rosenthal and Jacobson indicate that:

- raising teacher expectations has a positive effect on the performance of children;
- the effects are stronger with younger children;
- the effects are stronger with children from minority groups; and
- the effects decay with time.

Insights from chaos theory

Rosenthal and Jacobson's results challenged the assumption that the effects persisted, even for young children. The authors commented at the time was that 'they could not say why that was the case'. However, nearly thirty years later, new ideas from a different theory base can offer new accounts of the phenomena.

Paul Van Geert (1994) has applied concepts and mathematical models from chaos theory to look at learning *cycles*. Chaos theory does not actually describe random events, but makes a distinction between random and complex phenomena. There are four necessary and sufficient conditions to be met for non-linear or *chaotic* growth:

1 Learning is an iterative process; the output from one learning cycle acts as the input for the next.

2 At least three (but ideally lots more) items competing for the attention of the learner.

3 Attention is a finite commodity; if you are attending to one thing, you are attending less to another.

4 There are no large-scale, predetermined forces or architectures which determine what is learned.

If these conditions are met, then there will be non-linear growth. This will be characterised by periods of stability followed by rapid change, delayed effects of teaching, sensitivity to initial conditions and lack of predictability.

One element of this that is relevant to the Rosenthal and Jacobson findings is the possibility of *interest cycles.* There are three stages:

1 Interest contagion – At the beginning of an initiative, the pupil (or teacher) is excited by the novelty of the new material and finds increasing opportunities to practise the skill or apply the knowledge. The subject's interest is contagious and directs their attention to finding new applications. Each trial provides another opportunity to learn, so the rate of learning goes up – we see *accelerated learning.*

2 Saturation – The subject is interested in this new element for a limited time, after which the novel opportunities become exhausted and the learning *slows down.*

3 Recovery – The subject turns their attention to other things and stops practising the skill or acquiring the knowledge. Learning of this particular skill seems to *stop completely*. It will require a certain length of time before the subject becomes interested in this area again.

If we accept that this model may have applications here, we can see a possible cycle for the children. At the beginning, the teachers were interested in the potential accelerated growth for the selected children and may have spent more time encouraging them. This interest waned and the new teachers were unaware of the target group. This resulted in the children finding that they were not the subjects of increased attention and found other things to interest them. Clearly this is speculative, but it would account for the observations.

Possible mechanisms

The evidence seems clear. The expectations of teachers *do* influence the performance of children, albeit in quite complex ways. What are the possible processes that might account for this? We will consider how different psychological theories may be used to answer this question.

Behavioural psychology

Rosenthal and Jacobson's results were obtained by taking children's scores from written tests which were constructed by starting with easy questions and progressing to increasingly more difficult or challenging ones. Typically, a child experiences questions that they can answer with some ease, followed by those that they cannot. When the child experiences the more challenging ones, there are a variety of responses possible. The child might sit and think for a while, might guess, might ignore the question and move on. There are others. A teacher may have an idea of what the child is capable of. When selecting questions in the normal course of teaching, the teacher may match the question to the idea of the capability of the child. The child is rewarded by the teacher for getting the question correct. If the child is expected to be able to answer more difficult questions, the teacher may wait for the answer and reward the child for spending time on the question. Thus the child is rewarded for spending more time on the problem. Conversely, a teacher who holds the idea that a child is unlikely to be able to answer more challenging questions may limit the questions to easier ones. The child is rewarded for answering the easier ones and not for persevering with the harder ones. When the child is placed in a class test, they apply the previously rewarded behaviour to the new setting. Children who have been rewarded for persevering may persevere with the more difficult test items and raise their total score.

Therefore assumptions that children will not perform well are dangerous. This theory is strong in suggesting that children will perform differently in different contexts. Positive expectations, linked with systematic rewards for high performance, are key elements for obtaining the best results from children.

Cognitive psychology

When a child is questioned, s/he may know the answer well. Giving the appropriate response may be almost automatic, it may not involve acquiring new knowledge or practising a new skill. Lev Vygotsky described children having *zones of proximal development* (ZPD). Learning involves a change of psychological processes in which language plays a leading part. Children learn through the help of teachers who extend children's thinking by prompting using language. However, the type of problem accessible to the prompted child needs not to be much more complex than one which is solvable by the child alone. Problems which are too easy do not extend the child and neither do problems which are too difficult (or require excessive prompting). So the teacher, by estimating the child's ZPD, is instrumental in teaching new thinking skills. If a teacher underestimates the child's cognitive skills (and ZPD) the child will not receive questions that are effective teaching tools. Similarly, a teacher whose expectations are higher may be more effective *provided that the expectations are within the ZPD*. Simply raising expectations to unrealistic levels may actually *reduce* the effective teaching for that child. The Rosenthal and Jacobson study may have been less effective if they had suggested extremely large increases in cognitive abilities for their children.

Social constructionist psychology

When we consider the images that children have of themselves, we must include assessments of themselves as learners in a class. If children see themselves as successful, any information that challenges this may cause anxiety. The converse is also possible. The mental *scripts* can be:

> I am a good learner . . .
> Good learners do well in tests . . .
> therefore I will do well in this test . . .
> therefore I will try hard

or

> I am a poor learner . . .
> Poor learners always do badly in tests . . .
> therefore I will do badly in this test . . .
> therefore why bother to try.

An interesting insight into this can be obtained quite quickly by a teacher working with a child and is described by Van Geert (1994). Reading tests tend to start with easy items. The further the test goes, the harder the materials become. So a child's first experience of the test is usually success. However, it is possible to reverse the test so that the child starts with the hardest items, so the child's first experience is that of frustration and failure. As the items get easier, you might expect the point at which the child starts to get the items correct is the same as that found when the child is given the test from easy to hard. However, this is not the case. Children score more correct if the items are presented from easy to hard than the other way round. The child forms a mental representation of themselves in this test based on early experiences of the test items. The importance of selection of early experiences of success for children is clear from these ideas.

Implications for the classroom

Each of the schools of psychology outlined earlier leads to different theories of why (and how) children learn to act. There is a wide range of approach in schools and a great deal of eclecticism, with schools using elements from different psychological theories. At this stage we will outline the dimensions and illustrate each approach with examples found in schools. A fuller account is to be found in Chapter 6.

Biological psychology

As detailed in Chapter 1, explanations of children's behaviour fall into two categories, *causal* and *functional*. Children have biological needs for warmth, food, company and security. Maslow's hierarchy of needs (see Chapter 5) describes an order in which needs will be pursued by children. Children who are hungry are less likely to see beauty in art as they are motivated by food. Children whose basic biological needs are met are more likely to be motivated by the desire for cognitive growth and stimulation. Biological differences in children can account for differences in behaviour. The suggestion of a disorder can lead to medication.

Let us illustrate this with an example from a leading source of ideas based in biology – *The Diagnostic and Statistical Manual of Mental Disorders* (Fourth Edition) (DSM-IV). The authors describe *Oppositional Defiant Disorder* (ODD). The condition is found in children below nine or ten years and is defined as follows:

the *presence* of markedly defiant, disobedient, provocative behaviour and by the absence of more severe dissocial or aggressive acts that violate the law or rights of others ... Children with this disorder tend frequently and actively to defy adult requests or rules and deliberately to annoy other people. Usually they tend to be angry, resentful, and easily annoyed by other people whom they blame for their own mistakes or difficulties. Frequently, this behaviour is most evident in interactions with adults or peers whom the child knows well, and signs of the disorder may not be evident during a clinical interview.

The manual proceeds to describe both medical and psycho-social treatments. There is a description of the use of stimulant medication and the success rates of individual psychotherapy (low). Family therapy, the authors indicate, has not been properly researched.

If the adults around the child hold essentially biological models they point to the use of drugs or an acceptance that the children are constitutionally made this way. Changing the belief systems or management regimes do not suggest themselves. Medical management of children's behaviour is controversial and the rates of use vary in different cultures. Adults using this way of thinking about children are less likely to highlight their own roles in determining the behaviour of children.

Fairness and biology

The concept of *fairness* seems universal and of great importance for children, it underpins notions of consistency in management of pupils. It does not, however, appear to be a great subject of empirical research. If fairness is considered important across cultures the biological school of psychology suggests that it serves a useful purpose for promoting the species. What would add weight to this argument would be evidence of fairness as a concept in another species. In 2005 tentative evidence of human-like responses to unfairness was published about chimpanzees (Platt 2005). The study looked at the behaviours of chimpanzees which hadn't been together long. For a chimp, a grape is a valued item while a cucumber is less so. Chimps were given tokens that they could exchange for food. Chimps who had seen another chimp receive a grape for the token refused to take the cucumber, preferring to keep the token. This cannot be accounted for by classical learning theories which would predict that as the cucumber was still a reward, the chimps should exchange the token, so another process must be taking place.

The study also looked at the responses in very mature chimp groups. One group had been together for 30 years and the findings differed. The mature-group chimps did not refuse the cucumber. The researchers describe the older social group as having a 'tightly knit social structure characterised by intense social integration . . . [the unfairness] barely caused a ripple'. The tolerance of unfairness grew with increasing social closeness. This may be found to be true for families and friends. If these findings are replicated and generalised to human groups we have a model for understanding the importance of perceived fairness at the beginning of a school year when new social groups are forming.

Psychodynamic psychology

Behaviour is driven by unseen drives and needs. The early experiences of childhood influence and shape our behaviours and emotions, even into later life. They shape our personalities. The application of these ideas can be found in nurture groups and is described in Chapter 2.

An additional example can be found in a special school run by the National Children's Home in the Cotswolds. They have constructed a curriculum around the theories of D.W. Winnicott. The school:

> exists to provide a safe, holistic, caring and healing environment that enables children and young people who have experienced severe disruption and emotional trauma in the early years of their lives to recover, learn and grow toward maturity.

The programme is described thus:

> The cornerstone of treatment is the formation of a deep and trusting relationship between a child and a grown-up, which needs to provide a sufficient feeling of safety to enable the child to regress to the point of emotional arrest . . . [The school] seeks to offer stable adult relationships, based on psychodynamic principles, that enable boys to benefit from the carefully planned education and care services that are offered.
>
> (*Special Schools in Britain* 2005–6, p.43)

Adults who use this way of thinking generally consider that children can grow and improve, given the appropriate therapy. A danger arises if the adult is unsure of what psychotherapy can and cannot offer. It is very easy to look at a child and think that they 'need therapy'. Decontexualised therapy may be of value for many pupils, but it does not usually result in better classroom behaviour.

Social constructionist psychology

Recall that we consider the ways in which children see themselves as central to understanding behaviour. We highlight the development of the image of self through the interactions the child has with significant others.

A powerful insight into the thoughts of a child can be found in an account of a pupil from a special school in Chicago run by Bruno Bettelheim. The former pupil reflected on his behaviour at school. He was middle-aged at the time of the interview:

> As I arrived at the Orthogenic School, Patty was the one who greeted me, and I knew, as children know, I guess, that this lady liked me. But knowing that didn't make me happy. What had to happen was the process of testing. And with the kind of hatred I had for women, at that stage of my life, that process became very graphic. The fellow who had a parent who is sometimes nice and sometimes horrible begins to think that that's the way the world is. In my own case that's the way it was. At the time when I came to the school, as I was confronted with Patty, who was an exceptionally fine human being, and a very affectionate and decent human being, I wasn't able to accept the affection, which caused even more anger. Every human being wants to accept affection. But if you condition yourself to not accepting affection because if by accepting it you only let yourself in for the next downfall, you put yourself in a position where, by accepting it, you're asking for your own destruction. So you find yourself in a position where you

don't dare to hope that the affection is for real and you keep testing to find out if it is for real. That's the process whereby, step by step, you find out whether it is. Maybe that explains my own need to hurt those who would be nice, because in that environment, I needed to find out whether or not the affection would continue.

(Greenhalgh 1994)

The interventions developed from the social constructivist school include offering positive, affirming, accepting messages to children.

Implications for children of adults' beliefs

The beliefs or theories that adults hold lead to different courses of action. There are many examples found in the literature. Consider this comment from a miner's wife in the late 1950s:

> I think a child shouldn't wet his bed after he's three; if he does, he should get smacked for it. That one's three this month, and wets the bed *every* night. Well, we're only waiting for the twenty-seventh; after that she'll get smacked every time she does it, same as him [four-year-old].

(Newson and Newson 1963, p.200)

Compare it with the comment from a lorry-driver's wife from the same time: 'I haven't much time for training, I'm afraid. I just leave it to nature and let nature take its course' (ibid.: 125).

This approach highlights the need for children to receive positive messages about themselves. Children who have received strong messages that they are 'bad' are likely to live up to that name. If children arrive at school with that self-image, they can be confused if they are told that they are 'good'. The thoughts can be:

> My mum says I'm naughty.
> I get told off if I behave in a certain way.
> At school I get praised if I do as I am told.
> Good boys/girls get praised.
> I am not good.
> Therefore, the teacher has got it wrong.
> I must show them what I am really like.
> I will misbehave so that I get told off.

Clearly this is unsatisfactory for the school staff. It is also tempting to fall into the trap of not praising the child ('they can't handle praise'), but quiet, gentle encouragement on a personal basis will help the child to distinguish between the sense of self at home and that found in school. The belief held by the teacher that it is possible for the child to be different at home and school is essential if the teacher is to continue the programme.

Conclusion

The evidence seems to support the thesis that the beliefs and theories that adults hold about children will affect the ways in which they behave with them. The importance of the perception of fairness in children may be quite primitive in origin. We will end with an example of the possible differences of approaches of different groups working in the education system.

Practical example

The following case was presented to different individuals working with children with behavioural difficulties. The case is fictional, but made up of three cases known to one of the authors. The participants were either teachers in a unit for excluded children, teachers working in a behaviour support service or educational psychologists.

CASE STUDY

Sam is nine years old. His mother took drugs and drank heavily during pregnancy. He was born eight weeks prematurely, and spent his first three months of life in a special care baby unit. When he was discharged he was taken into care. Initially he was placed with very experienced short-term foster carers. Unfortunately, they were unable to keep him after a year and he went to different carers. He was finally adopted at the age of three. While in foster care he went to a playgroup, but he was described as 'difficult' with other children. The playgroup leader asked the carer to keep him at home until he had settled more. His adopted parents sent him to a nursery, but they, too, said that he was not relating to the other children and was hurting them, although they said that they didn't think that he meant to hurt them. He was trying to play. His parents were offered a place in a special nursery, which catered for children from a wide range of backgrounds. There were many children there was did not relate well to others.

Sam was sent to his local primary school. The school was aware that he had not been able to go to a local nursery. He did not know the other children of the school, although they had already had a year together and knew each other. They were very good with him and helped him to join in the local activities both in and out of school. However, his teachers did describe him as 'very active' and 'always on the go'. They noticed that he did not like reading and preferred to play in the home corner rather than listen to a story. At the age of 9 he had the reading skills of the average six-year-old. He was still finding it difficult to sit still in class and occasionally got into trouble for hitting other pupils. The head teacher suggested that the staff and parents might like to talk to a psychologist/support teacher. They agreed.

The staff were asked the following questions: If this case was presented to you, what would be your starting points? What priorities would you have for Sam? What would you consider to be a successful outcome?

We will consider the three different groups, starting with three teachers in the unit for excluded children. For the psychologists we include a statement of their professional orientation.

Teachers from a unit for excluded pupils

Table 3.1   Views of teachers from a unit for excluded pupils

Teacher	Starting points	Priorities	Successful outcome
1	Want to go out to see him	Introduce him to circle time	Sam being happy and accessing the curriculum
2	Get my own impressions	Increase his reading age	Improvement in reading age and a reduction in the problems of hitting
3	Talk to him one-to-one	Find ways for Sam to gain real friendships	Can manage to stay in the classroom and interact with other pupils without hurting them

Teachers from a behaviour support service

Table 3.2   Views from teachers from a behaviour support service

Teacher	Starting points	Priorities	Successful outcome
1	Want to get as much background as I can	Develop his social skills	Sam being happy and progressing with reading and education
2	An assessment of his literacy difficulties	Access funding to further his literacy and increase his friendship group	To increase his literacy skills within one year of his peers or beyond. Before and after comparisons using checklists.

Educational psychologists

Table 3.3   View of educational psychologists

Psychologist and preferred orientation	Starting points	Priorities	Successful outcome
1. Psychodynamic/ ecosystemic	Acceptance of my own emotional responses. Gather information about background.	Consider attachment style (see Bowlby). Look at the attachments he has in school. Look carefully at transitions.	Greater understanding of this boy's real needs which include emotional containment, so that he may feel safe enough to take the risks associated with learning

2. Cognitive	Hypothesis that he has missed out and hasn't developed learning how to learn skills	Underlying thinking and processing skills	Accelerated reading and improved attention and listening
3. Humanist	Gain clear understanding of how Sam felt about his own learning	Self-esteem, building confidence and having a sense that he can succeed	Sam has a positive sense of himself as a learner, positive relationships with peers and is able to reflect on the areas he finds difficult
4. Behavioural	Gather information about rewards and corrections used for behaviour and learning. Check match between existing skills and demands of the tasks.	Ensure that Sam is receiving clear indications of expectations and rewards for good behaviour and learning.	Sam gains friends following reduction in behavioural incidents, gains in reading skills and is happy in school.

Note the differences, particularly within the psychologists. The kind of approach adopted arises from the theories that the individuals have and the hypotheses generated by the professionals.

The intention here is not to offer value judgements. Each school of psychology has its own strengths and weaknesses. By understanding the different theories used by the adults, we can understand the differences in approach. However, practical applications of theories do need to stand up to evaluation. Only by understanding the different theories will we begin to understand how to evaluate the outcomes of their application.

Summary

Teachers are required to have high expectations for their children. The question can be asked 'Why?'. Surely a more reasonable position might be to have *realistic* expectations for children. What this chapter has presented is some of the evidence that the expectations held by adults are not isolated thoughts in their minds. They shape the way we behave towards children and can influence educational and personal outcomes for those children. In extreme circumstances, simply changing expectations in adults can change performance in tests. The mechanisms may not be well understood, but the findings are clear.

We hope that this chapter has presented evidence that:

- we develop theories about children;
- these theories are subject to factors which can lead to unreliable conclusions;
- the theories have an impact on educational outcomes for children;
- changing our theories about children can change the educational outcomes for those children.

CHAPTER 4

Classroom learning and learning styles

Introduction and chapter aims

Trends and fashions in education come and go with what often seems to be alarming rapidity. It is often difficult to keep up with the pace of change in education. However, one constant is that learning is a central aspect of education. The concept of *value added* assumes that it is possible to measure the difference that a school has made to its pupils. If we accept that this concept is to be used in making judgements about schools, we are saying that we should be able to see some change in pupils over the time that they attend school. This notion is the basis of what learning is about; that is, it involves some kind of change.

Psychology has a great deal to say about learning. There are a number of theories that have practical application in the classroom and which will be examined in this chapter. The specific aims of the chapter are:

- to examine a variety of theories of learning that can be applied in the classroom; and
- to examine ways in which theories of learning can help teachers to use effective teaching methods that promote independent learning.

What do we mean by learning?

This might seem like a strange starting point. Surely we all know what learning is about? But do we? Think about the following statement:

'I learned French at school thirty years ago. If I went to France for my holidays I could probably "get by" but I don't think I would have much to show for the five years I spent learning the language. I did enough to pass my exam at school, that's all. I don't think the way the subject was taught was very effective. All I remember doing was learning long lists of French words. It all seemed pretty meaningless. Perhaps things would be different now because we know so much more about how our brains work, so I guess that might have made a difference to how the subject was taught.'

This statement says a number of things about learning. An analogy of a jigsaw has been chosen as it demonstrates the way in which a number of parts fit together in order to make a whole picture. We will therefore identify the jigsaw pieces that are aspects of learning.

Has this person learned? Clearly, something has 'stuck', since they feel that they could 'get by'. Some permanent change has taken place if the individual is able to speak some French when they could not do so at all before commencing French lessons. This statement also says something about memory. Is learning simply about remembering and forgetting? We have two pieces to our 'learning jigsaw' that will help to make up a picture of what learning is: it involves change and it involves remembering.

What do you think would have happened to this person's proficiency in French if they had taken a holiday in France every year since learning the subject at school? It is possible that more of the language would have been retained as it was in fairly frequent use. Therefore, the third piece of our 'learning jigsaw' is about the role of repetition and rehearsal in learning.

The statement relates to a subject in the curriculum. It does not mention how the individual learned. He/she must have used some thought processes in order to learn French. For example, s/he would need to have made sense of auditory information when hearing the teacher speaking French. The next part of our learning jigsaw, therefore, is that learning is about *how* as well as *what* we learn.

Our learner comments about the way the subject was taught. Here, then, is another piece of the jigsaw: the relationship between learning and instruction. This area might also include a consideration of *learning styles*.

Finally, our learner wonders whether things might be different today because we understand more about the function of the brain. This is an important consideration in our examination of learning, since there are many popular initiatives based on assumptions and knowledge about the way in which the brain works. Therefore, the subject of *neuroscience* and its relationship to education should be considered.

Memory

Cognitive psychology studies mental processes; it attempts to describe the mind and how it works. Memory is a major area of study for cognitive psychologists. Memory is the way in which we encode, store and retrieve information. Encoding is the process by which information is transformed to memory. Initially, we receive information in the form of a range of stimuli; for example, auditory (something we hear) or visual (something we see). In order for information to be encoded, the learner needs to pay attention. Therefore, attention is a prerequisite for memory, otherwise the stimuli presented will not be encoded. Attention is a process for either focusing on or ignoring information. There are a number of theories in cognitive psychology relating to attention. These theories either emphasise a filtering system (e.g. Broadbent 1958) or a selection system, where important and relevant information is recognised and then selected (e.g. Deutsch and Deutsch 1963).

Hermann Ebbinghaus (1850–1909) was one of the first psychologists to study memory. His findings are still relevant. Ebbinghaus invented 2,300 nonsense syllables in order to investigate memory and recall. He compared the process of memorising nonsense material with that of meaningful material and found that much less effort is required to memorise meaningful material. He introduced three key ideas about memory that remain important: the learning curve; overlearning; and serial position. Ebbinghaus's experiments showed that recall increases as the number of repetitions increase. He called this the learning curve. Overlearning is a process where learning continues even after a correct performance. Ebbinghaus demonstrated that when this happens, the likelihood of forgetting is reduced significantly, and recall can take place even when the learner is under stress. Serial position refers to the effect of the position of information in a list on recall. Ebbinghaus's experiments showed that it is more likely that an individual will recall information at the beginning and end, rather than in the middle. He called these effects *primacy* (at the beginning) and *recency* (at the end). This effect is seen during free recall; that is, when recall of a list of information does not have to be in the same order that it was presented.

One of the main models for looking at how memory works is an information processing model that divides memory into long- and short-term memory. Miller (1956) looked at short-term memory and suggested that 'chunking' information helps to increase capacity. That is, more information can be processed when it is linked together rather than presented as separate 'bits'. Miller suggested that the average capacity of short-term memory is seven units of information, plus or minus two.

Atkinson and Shiffrin (1968) also suggested an information processing model that has three stages: sensory; short-term memory (STM); and long-term memory (LTM). They suggested that information is retained in the STM using strategies such as categorising, sequencing, relevance and relationship to other knowledge. Transfer to LTM involves elaboration (a range of mental processes that aid storage, such as visualisation or making connections with other objects or words) and distributed practice (reviewing learning).

The term *working memory* is one that you might encounter. Working memory is a combination of short-term memory and attention and involves the storage of one piece of information while another, related, piece is being processed. An example of this might be a mental maths calculation.

The concept of schema is an aspect of theories about memory that should be examined. In relation to memory, a schema is a mental model or problem-solving skill (in contrast to facts or knowledge). Sweller (1988) combines the concept of schema with research into STM. He proposes that the capacity of working memory can be increased by use of schema. If we have effective problem-solving strategies, we can handle more information in our working memory. Sweller uses this model to distinguish between an expert and a novice. An expert has well-developed schema that enable him/her to deal with information in working memory more efficiently. Sweller suggests that working memory should not be overloaded as this will prevent schema from being formed.

Memory: implications for classroom practice

An information processing view of learning describes learning as the process whereby information is encoded into short-term memory and then transferred into long-term memory. Therefore, teaching is the means by which this process is facilitated. It was stated that attention is the prerequisite for this process. Therefore, the first implication for the classroom is related to attention. If you do not have the full attention of your pupils, then it is unlikely that information will be encoded to their short-term memory. If this does not happen, then there will be no transfer to long-term memory. Although psychological theory suggests that there are mechanisms for filtering and/or selecting information, these processes can be assisted by ensuring that pupils are not bombarded with too many stimuli, or that there are not competing demands for attention in the classroom. This might seem obvious; however, the authors' experiences of observing classrooms over a number of years would suggest that these points are worth highlighting. For example, we have seen teachers trying to give task instructions before making sure that s/he has the attention of the whole class, or a teacher trying to teach a whole-class lesson while a classroom assistant repeats what has been said to a small group in the class. Therefore, the main messages are to minimise distractions. Make sure that you are the only one talking and check that you have gained everyone's attention before you begin any instructions or explanations needed by the whole class. Many teachers use signals or cues in order to indicate to their pupils that they need to stop and listen.

Many of the theories discussed contain some reference to *connections*. Effective and efficient processing, transfer and retrieval can be assisted by links to prior learning. An example cited in the preceding section involved the role of categorisation in aiding retention in short-term memory. The ability to categorise can be likened to a mental 'filing cabinet'. If I am presented with some new information, I can make sense of it more easily by linking it to a group or set. For example, if I see something with four legs and a tail that makes a 'woof' sound, I can put this into a category called 'dogs', even if I do not know the specific breed. An implication for classroom practice is that linking new information to prior knowledge and experience will assist retention in short-term memory and transfer to long-term memory. This idea of 'connections' in learning is the basis for subsumption theory of David Ausabel (1963). The concept of subsumption involves the learner assimilating new information into existing cognitive structures, or schema. Therefore, this theory of learning fits in with the idea of schema as being part of the process of memory. Ausabel's theory of learning introduced the concept of an *advance organiser*. An advance organiser is a mechanism for linking new and prior learning and can take the form of an expository organiser (where reference is made to main or superordinate categories; in the example of categorisation given above, this would be the category of 'animals') or a comparative organiser (where analogies are used to introduce new material, an example being comparing the brain with a computer).

THEORY AND PRACTICE LINKS

Advance organisers, making connections

Here are some examples of the way in which connections and advance organisers might be used in the classroom:

In *History*: The concept of kingship or the divine right of kings might be used as a means of introducing new material about the reign of specific monarchs. For younger children, the idea of a 'king' might be taught, then used to introduce new material about, for example, Henry VIII.

In *Maths*: Relationships between the four rules (for example, how multiplication and division are related), or number facts about a given number (for example, 10 can be expressed as 6+4 or 7+3).

In *Chemistry*: Teaching the structure of an atom by an analogy with the solar system (the nucleus is like the sun and the electron revolves around it, just as the Earth revolves around the Sun).

Now choose some new material that you are going to teach. Note down an advance organiser. Note down the prior learning that this new material relates to. Include this information in your lesson planning.

Actions to take account of, that have implications for the classroom, are suggested as follows:

- Be aware of primacy and recency effects when planning lessons. If you are presenting complex information, do this at the beginning and/or end of the lesson.

- Give opportunities for overlearning. Don't just accept one or two instances of correct recall. Give time for additional practice in order to maximise the chances of future recall. These opportunities can be applied to learning information such as number facts, spelling, word recognition, letter–sound recognition, maths or chemistry formulae.

- Think about the amount of information you present. Remember that there is a maximum of nine units of information that can be processed at any one time.

- Sequence information in a logical order.

- Pay attention to rehearsal and repetition. Distributed practice means that little and often is the most effective means of rehearsal.

- Present information verbally *and* visually.

THEORY AND PRACTICE LINKS

Applying theories of memory

You will need a lesson plan for this activity.

In your lesson plan, add the following subheadings that relate to application of theories about memory. Under each heading, note down what action you will take.

How pupil attention will be gained

Complex information (if applicable)

Overlearning opportunities (if applicable)

Number of units of information to be presented

Sequence of presentation of information

How information will be rehearsed and repeated

Verbal and visual presentation

Repetition and rehearsal

The section about memory has already highlighted the importance of repetition and rehearsal. In this section, we will examine a particular theory of learning in order to look more closely at these aspects.

The example of our French learner suggested that one of the reasons they had forgotten much of the French learned was due to lack of use. Therefore, the amount and type of repetition and rehearsal were important elements in retention. The section on memory has already suggested that distributed practice (that is, little and often) is an effective strategy and that overlearning helps to decrease the likelihood of forgetting. But how much repetition is needed? How will we know that learning has occurred and that it will be retained?

The Learning Hierarchy (Haring 1978) can help to answer the questions in the previous paragraph. The steps in the hierarchy are described in Table 4.1.

Repetition and rehearsal: implications for teaching

The learning hierarchy can be applied to any aspect of teaching that involves skills performed by the learner. It helps learners to develop a skill to a level of fluency that ensures retention. Putting the hierarchy into practice means that you should pay attention to the speed with which a pupil performs a skill, as well as the

Table 4.1   Haring and Eaton's Learning Hierarchy

Stage of hierarchy	What it means	Example	What the teacher should do
Acquisition	A new skill is introduced to the pupil. The pupil learns how to perform the skill with few errors but cannot yet perform the skill with any speed.	The pupil learns to recognise five new sight words. The pupil can read all five words correctly but it takes a long time to do so. Performance is hesitant.	Model or demonstrate the new skill. Give opportunities for rehearsal until a correct performance is observed (but at this stage there is no need to focus on speed).
Fluency	The pupil is able to perform the skill accurately and with speed. At this stage, the teacher might set a criterion for fluency that will make sure that the skill is mastered (that is, it is likely to be retained). In the case of word recognition, an acceptable level of fluency for skill mastery would be to read 50 words correctly in a minute.	The pupil reads the five words at the set level of fluency.	Provide opportunities for further practice which emphasises fluency.
Maintenance	The pupil is able to retain the skill over time.	The pupil can read five words in the same setting without further specific tuition.	Pupil has opportunities to practise without specific adult direction.
Generalisation	The pupil is able to use the skill in novel situations. The pupil can discriminate between the target skill and similar skills.	The pupil is able to read the five words when they are presented in sentences. The pupil can discriminate the five words from other words that look or sound alike.	Present the five words in a number of different formats. Remind the pupil about use of the target skill when a new presentation is used. Continue to give periodic opportunities to practise the skill.

(continued)

Table 4.1 Continued

Stage of hierarchy	What it means	Example	What the teacher should do
Adaptation	The pupil can apply the new skill to novel settings without reminders from the teacher.	The pupil is able to read the five sight words in a range of different texts (e.g. newspaper, reading book, worksheet, maths problem).	Make sure that the words are included in a range of texts used in class.

accuracy. This means that opportunities for practice and rehearsal should be built in to medium- and long-term planning.

Finding out more about applying the learning hierarchy

Precision teaching is a way of evaluating both accuracy and fluency in skill performance. You can find out more by:

- contacting your LEA Educational Psychology Service;
- looking at the website of the Standard Celeration Society (www.celeration.org);
- looking at resources on the Teacher Resource exchange website (www.tre.ngfl.gov.uk); and
- reading Chapter 7 of *Psychology for Teaching Assistants* (Arnold and Yeomans 2005).

The processes of learning

Processes of learning are concerned with *how* we learn rather than *what* we learn. These processes are sometimes referred to as *thinking skills* or *learning to learn skills*. In 1998, the Department for Education and Employment commissioned research into thinking skills. Carol McGuiness (1999), from Queen's University Belfast carried out a review and evaluation.

Later government documentation and guidance has made much more explicit reference to thinking skills. The Qualifications and Curriculum Authority (QCA) has identified a range of thinking skills that are promoted as 'learning across the curriculum'. Table 4.2 shows the major categories of thinking skills identified by QCA, together with the description of the range of skills involved in each category.

The work of Professor Reuven Feurstein will be examined in detail in order to identify the psychological underpinnings of ideas about thinking skills.

Reuven Feurstein was a pupil of Jean Piaget. After the Second World War, he obtained a job that involved assessing adolescent immigrants to the newly created

Table 4.2 QCA thinking skills

Main category	Description of associated skills
Information processing skills	Locate and collect relevant information; sort, classify, sequence, compare, contrast and analyse part/whole relationships.
Reasoning skills	Give reasons for opinions and actions, draw inferences and make deductions, use precise language to explain what the pupils think and make judgements and decisions informed by reasons or evidence.
Enquiry skills	Ask relevant questions; pose and define problems; plan what to do next and how to research; predict outcomes and anticipate responses; test conclusions and improve ideas.
Creative thinking skills	Generate and extend ideas; suggest hypotheses; apply imagination; and look for alternative innovative outcomes.
Evaluation skills	Evaluate information; judge the value of what the pupils read, hear and do; develop criteria for judging the value of their own and others' work and for having confidence in their judgements.

state of Israel, in order to determine the most suitable type of schooling for them. He used intelligence tests in order to do this. However, the results were puzzling. A very large number of the young people tested obtained low scores, indicating that they had low intelligence. Feurstein could not accept that these results were a true reflection of the young people's abilities, so he set out to find other explanations for the results. The immigrants fell into two main categories: they were either Holocaust survivors, or they came from very different cultures (for example, many immigrants came from north Africa). Feurstein suggested that these factors would account for the low IQ scores. The Holocaust survivors had experienced *cultural deprivation*, that is they had been deprived of their culture due to the death of family members who would transmit that culture, and they were traumatised by their experience of the Holocaust. The second group of young people had experienced *cultural difference*, where they had received adequate transmission of their culture but were now expected to function in a different culture. The experience of this difference was, Feurstein argued, the reason for low scores in the tests administered.

The two factors described above led Feurstein to propose that intelligence was not fixed. He described intelligence as *cognitive flexibility and adaptability*. The newly arrived immigrants had not yet had an opportunity to adapt to their new environment, but were being tested using the standards and values of this new environment. Therefore it is little wonder that they performed badly. This experience led to the formulation of the theory of *structural cognitive modifiability* (Feurstein *et al.* 2002). Essentially, this theory states that cognitive functioning can change irrespective of age, aetiology (causes) and severity. These three factors are seen as challenges rather than barriers to learning. The way in which change is brought about is via mediation. As noted in Chapter 2, mediation is a particular way of learning where the learner does not interact directly with stimuli, but instead has these stimuli filtered and interpreted. These processes of filtering and interpretation are part of mediation. A mediator helps the learner to make sense of the world. Through mediation, cognitive functions can be changed and improved. Mediation can be provided by a range of individuals. The first mediators are the child's parents and carers. Mediation can be provided by the community, as part of the transmission of culture. *Mediated Learning Experience* (MLE) brings about changes in cognitive functioning.

Feurstein's theories share common ground with those of Vygotsky, although at the time that Feurstein was developing his ideas Vygotsky's work was not known outside what was then the Soviet Union.

Feuerstein suggested that all individuals have a range of cognitive functions which are subject to change as a result of mediation. Feurstein's cognitive functions are the underlying skills needed for effective learning. They can be viewed as synonymous with the descriptors used earlier: thinking skills, process skills, and learning to learn skills. If you look back at Table 4.2 you will see many descriptors that are the same or similar.

Feurstein suggested that cognitive functions are observed in three phases: input, elaboration and output. Input is the phase of gathering information; elaboration is where the information is used; output is where the learner shows what s/he has learned.

Feurstein's theory of structural cognitive modifiability led to the development of a teaching programme called Instrumental Enrichment (IE). The IE programme is taught as a discrete subject; however, the use of mediation is a unique characteristic of its delivery that helps to ensure that learning is applied and generalised. This is due to the characteristics of mediation as described by Feurstein. One essential characteristic is called *transcendence*. This refers to generalisation and is sometimes called bridging. Links are made to other aspects of the pupils' lives, including their school and classroom experiences. Links are elicited from pupils by asking questions that begin with 'When else do we . . .?', or 'Where else do we . . .?'.

A full IE course can last up to two years, being delivered at least twice a week.

The processes of learning: implications for teaching

When considering the role of process skills (Promote active and independent learning that enables pupils to think for themselves, and to plan and manage their own learning), it is important to consider how to promote the processes as well as the products of learning.

There is much debate about the most effective way of teaching and promoting the processes of learning. Carol McGuiness's (1999) research suggested three models of delivery:

- as a separate subject on the timetable (an example of this would be Feurstein's Instrumental Enrichment programme);

- as part of a specific subject (an example of this would be a programme such as Cognitive Acceleration through Science Education (CASE) (Adey *et al.* 1995); and

- as a cross-curricular subject, where there is no separate timetable 'slot' but where all lessons contain an element of thinking skills.

We would suggest that the most pragmatic option would be the third, since you are unlikely to have sufficient control over the timetable to implement either of the first two approaches. It should be possible to teach and promote thinking skills in the classroom provided that care is taken to incorporate them at the planning stage. There are many ways in which the processes of learning can assist the learning of specific subjects or curriculum areas (see Table 4.3).

Table 4.3 QCA Thinking Skills, Feurstein's Cognitive Functions and Curriculum Applications

QCA	Feurstein	Curriculum application
Information processing skills Locate and collect relevant information, sort, classify, sequence, compare, contrast and analyse part/whole relationships.	Focused perception. Precision and accuracy (at the input stage). Systematic exploration. Planning behaviour. Comparative behaviour. Categorisation. Labelling. Interiorisation. Dealing with several sources of information (input and elaboration phases). Projecting relationships. Conservation of constancy.	Carry out a reading comprehension exercise where specific information has to be located from a prose passage. The passage will have to be looked at systematically and a comparison made with language of comprehension questions with that of the passage. Maths: sorting activities. Science: grouping objects into categories such as 'living' and 'not living'. History: compare two accounts of the same historical event.

(continued)

Table 4.3   Continued

QCA	Feurstein	Curriculum application
Reasoning skills Give reasons for opinions and actions, draw inferences and make deductions, use precise language to explain what they [pupils] think and make judgements and decisions informed by reasons or evidence.	Overcoming egocentric communication. Precision and accuracy (output phase). Logical evidence. Hypothetical thinking.	Be able to use and understand subject-specific language. English: Write a book review giving your opinion about the book and defending that opinion. Art: Express and defend an opinion about a particular work of art or genre.
Enquiry skills Ask relevant questions, pose and define problems, plan what to do next and how to research, predict outcomes and anticipate responses, test conclusions and improve ideas.	Defining the problem. Sequencing and planning behaviour (elaboration phase). Hypothetical thinking.	English: Draft a piece of written work with attention to sequence. Science: Make and test hypotheses (e.g. 'What will happen if my seeds are given light but not water?').
Creative thinking skills Generate and extend ideas, suggest hypotheses, apply imagination and look for alternative innovative outcomes.	Hypothetical thinking. Projecting relationships.	Music: What would happen if I changed the key/time/ instrumentation? Science: Make and test hypotheses.
Evaluation skills Evaluate information, judge the value of what they [pupils] read, hear and do, develop criteria for judging the value of their own and others' work and to have confidence in their judgements.	Hypothetical thinking. Logical evidence.	Human geography: Analyse and evaluate data from a project about shopping patterns.

Using this list, it is possible to begin to make links between curriculum content that you are teaching and the process skills that underpin the content. The application activity will help you to begin to plan your teaching.

THEORY AND PRACTICE LINKS

The processes of learning

Choose a cognitive function from the lists above.

Draw a mind map or web diagram showing what aspects of the taught curriculum this function can relate to. Make these links relevant to your teaching (it might relate to a specific subject that you teach all the time or to an aspect of the curriculum that you will be teaching in the near future).

Choose one or two curriculum links that you have identified and incorporate the teaching of the process skills into your lesson planning.

Use the MLE characteristic of transcendence. Make time to give examples of and elicit examples from pupils of applications of the process skill(s). Use the questions 'When else . . .?' and 'Where else . . .?' as a format.

Finding out more about thinking skills

Howard Sharron's book, *Changing Children's Minds*, is an excellent and very readable text about Feurstein's work. It is available from Questions Publishing, Leonard House, Digbeth, Birmingham B5 6ET (www.questionsonlinecatalogue. co.uk).

The International Centre for the Enhancement of Learning Potential website is useful (www.icelp.org).

Learning Across the Curriculum is a link that can be accessed from the QCA website (www.qca.org.uk).

The Hope Centre for Cognitive Education, located in London NW2, offers training in Instrumental Enrichment (www.hope-centre.org.uk).

Learning styles

The 'pen portrait' of the French learner at the beginning of this chapter hinted at the role of learning styles in the comment about the way in which the subject was taught. It could be inferred from the statement that the method of teaching did not match the way in which the learner learned. This brings us to a consideration of learning styles. A learning style is simply a set or repertoire of behaviours that we tend to use when we are learning something. Ellis (1985), for example, defines a learning style as 'how a person perceives, comprehends, organises and recalls information'. Learning-style theorists argue that we develop a preferred way of learning and tend to take a similar approach to tasks that we are presented with. Consequently, a theory about learning styles would say that learning is most likely to take place when teaching is aimed at the individual's learning style. There are a large number of theories and concepts related to learning styles. Research carried out by Professor Coffield on behalf of the Learning and Skills Development

Agency (LSDA), a government body that oversees the provision of post-16 education, identified 31 different theories and concepts, some of which were incompatible (Coffield *et al.* 2004).

The idea of a learning style is related to theories about personality. For example, Silver *et al.* (1997) suggest that personality is one of two common elements of any learning-style theory, the other being process (that is, how learning takes place). They note that in the 1920s, the psychologist Carl Jung suggested that there were differences in the ways in which individuals perceive the world, make decisions and think about their actions. Therefore, they trace the development of learning-style theory back to one of the earliest practitioners of psychology.

David Kolb (see, for example, Kolb 1984) is an influential voice in the learning styles arena. Many other theories are a variation of his basic model. Kolb suggests that there are four main styles of learning:

- Concrete experience (CE); where information is taken in through direct experience and learning is a very 'hands on' process;
- Reflective observation (RO); where learning is less active than in the concrete dimension, consisting of observing, gathering and analysing information;
- Active experimentation (AE); where learning involves finding practical solutions to problems; and
- Abstract conceptualisation (AC); where logic and abstract thought are a feature of learning.

Kolb's theory does not give any explicit recognition to the role of *affect* in learning; that is emotions and feelings. This dimension is reflected in Seagal and Horne's (1985) model, which adds aspects of affective and physical learning to Kolb's model.

Another conceptualisation of learning styles that you might come across is the concept of VAK learning. VAK stands for **V**isual, **A**uditory and **K**inaesthetic. This model of learning styles looks at the way in which learners receive information and suggests that one of the three information receiving channels might be dominant. Therefore, a learner who is predominantly auditory will prefer to receive information via the spoken word. A learner who is predominantly visual will prefer to receive information via the written word (visuo-linguistic) or via other visual means such as pictures or diagrams (visuo-spatial). A learner who is predominantly kinaesthetic will prefer to receive information via touch and/or movement.

Learning styles: implications for teaching

What sense should a busy class or subject teacher make of the issue of learning styles? The sources consulted for this chapter were high on theories and concepts but low on evidence. An emphasis on learning styles is in danger of leading practitioners down the road of 'within-child attribution', that is that learning (or not learning) is attributed to characteristics of the learner that are fixed, rather than taking account of the contexts and environments in which learning takes place (including the type and delivery of instruction, which can have a powerful effect on learning). There is also a danger that emphasis on learning styles lead to labelling learners, so that we might restrict opportunities (for example 'Jane is an auditory learner, so don't bother giving her anything to read').

A consideration of the role of learning styles in the classroom must take account of the practicalities of differentiating your teaching in order to ensure that your teaching is relevant and appropriate for a range of learning styles. Theories about learning style have generated a large number of inventories and questionnaires that purport to identify an individual's preferred style. However, a note of caution should be given here. Coffield *et al.*'s (2004) research examined a range of these instruments (more than seventy) and concluded that many of them had low reliability and validity; that is, they did not give consistent results with repeated use (reliability) and did not measure what they set out to measure (validity). In any case, time constraints might not permit you to administer an inventory to your pupils (especially if you are a subject teacher who might teach several sets of pupils during the course of a typical week). Perhaps the most pragmatic approach is to be aware of the range of different styles and to ensure that your lesson planning and delivery try to cover at least some of the range. For example, if you are introducing new information or concepts to a class, you can make sure that this is delivered via visual and auditory means. Try to balance task demands so that sometimes you use concrete experience and hands-on learning, and at other times reflection and logic. Mix 'open' and 'closed' questioning so that you are not always seeking a 'right' answer.

In conclusion, theories about learning styles give us some pointers about the different ways in which learners prefer to receive and process information. However, research evidence is weak and instruments designed to pinpoint differing learning styles have generally poor reliability and validity. It is probably not useful, therefore, to expend too much time and effort in trying to match your teaching to individual learning styles, assuming that you have time to find out what these are. Good teaching should, by definition, use a variety of means of presentation and delivery in order to engage and motivate pupils, and will therefore appeal to a range of preferred modes of learning.

The role of the brain

Advances in medical science and technology mean that it is possible to study the structure and function of the human brain in great detail. Techniques for scanning the brain, such as Magnetic Resonance Imaging (MRI) and Positron Emission

Tomography (PET) scanning, can now provide accurate pictures of brain activity, leading to the identification of specific areas of the brain that are responsible for aspects of the individual's learning and behaviour. The discipline of *neuroscience*, that is looking at the way in which the brain learns, has developed alongside these technological advances. As our understanding of the brain's structure and function has increased there have been more connections between neuroscience and education. For example, it is possible to see activity in specific areas of the brain when an individual is reading.

The structure and function of the brain: brief overview

The brain can be divided into three parts: the brain stem, the cerebellum and the cerebrum. The brain stem is often called the 'primitive brain' as this type of brain is found in all animals. In humans, this area of the brain is related to vision and hearing (the mid-brain), motor control and posture (the pons) and the maintenance of vital functions such as breathing and heart beat (the medulla). The cerebellum ('little brain') is associated with movement, posture and balance. The cerebrum is sometimes thought of as the 'higher brain'. This part of the brain is most developed in humans. It is divided into two hemispheres (left and right). The left hemisphere controls the right side of the body and vice versa. The hemispheres are connected by the corpus callosum. The cerebrum is divided into four lobes as follows:

The *frontal lobe* (problem solving, abstract thought, voluntary movement);

The *parietal lobe* (touch, understanding sensory information and some aspects of language and reading);

The *occipital lobe* (vision); and

The *temporal lobe* (hearing, auditory memory, memory in general, music and some aspects of speech and language).

Brain cells are the means by which messages are sent and received by the brain. There are two types of brain cell: *glial* cells and *neurons*. Glial cells carry nutrients and speed repairs. Neurons contain axons for sending information and dendrites for receiving information. They connect to each other via a synapse, which is a gap between two neurons. Messages are sent across synapses. Therefore a synapse is a junction between an axon of one neuron and a dendrite of another. Messages are sent across synapses by *neurotransmitters*. These are 'chemical messengers' that transport electrical signals from one neuron to another. Neurotransmitters can either excite or inhibit neuron activity. Examples of neurotransmitters are serotonin (which regulates emotion) and dopamine (which controls sensations of pleasure). The number of neurons remains fairly constant throughout an individual's life, but the number of synaptic connections is subject to change.

There are two processes that are important in the relationship between brain function and learning: *synaptogenesis* and *pruning*. Synaptogenesis is the process of forming new connections between neurons, and pruning involves removing weak contacts and strengthening others. The saying 'use it or lose it' can be applied to our brains; pruning can be triggered by lack of use.

The role of the brain: implications for teaching

Having looked briefly at the structure and function of the brain, we must now consider how to use this information in order to enhance and promote learning. Goswami (2004) comments:

> Learning broadly comprises changes in connectivity, either via changes in potentiation at the synapse or via the strengthening or pruning of connections. Successful teaching thus directly affects brain function by changing connectivity.

At the beginning of this chapter it was noted that learning involves change. The view of learning derived from neuroscience is that this change takes place at the 'micro' level of the synaptic connections being made within the brain. However, we should be cautious when thinking about how this should influence our teaching. Although it is possible to identify the changes that take place within areas of the brain associated with different aspects of learning or skills, it is quite another matter to be able to deliver teaching that we *know* will impact on brain structure or which will produce activity in specified areas of the brain. In recent years there has been an increase in so-called 'brain based learning' that purports to make explicit links between what we know about brain function and structure, and teaching. The problem with these links is that a great deal of the research evidence on which these approaches are based is derived from studies of animals, or from university-based studies where the subjects are undergraduates. Therefore, generalisation of findings is problematic.

Goswami identifies three 'neuromyths' that are prevalent in educational circles. She defines a neuromyth as a process where neurological information is applied inappropriately to education. The three that she identifies are:

Left- and right-brain differences: Some interventions claims to 'connect up' the two halves of the brain. Goswami points out that there are connections between both hemispheres and that neuro-imaging shows that both hemispheres are active when specific tasks are performed. The implication of this neuromyth is that educational programmes claiming to make connections between the hemispheres should be viewed with extreme caution.

Critical periods: Many educationalists claim that there are critical periods for brain development and that if the opportunity is missed, learning will never take place. Goswami prefers to use the term 'optimal periods', suggesting that there might be periods where learning is most likely to take place but that a missed opportunity does not mean that the chance of learning is lost forever. Hall (2005) points out that research into critical periods has been carried out with cats and monkeys, not humans.

Enriched environments: Some theories that stress the effect of environmental influences on brain development advocate enriched environments in order to promote brain development. However, this is a neuromyth because most of the studies have been carried out with rats. There is evidence that the environment can lead to new connections being made in the brain. However, Goswami points out that the effect of the environment should not be related to predictions about the individual's capacity to learn.

The main message about the role of the brain in learning is to be cautious. Although there is no doubt that the brain is involved in learning, there is little evidence that particular teaching methods or strategies have a direct effect on brain structure or function. You cannot know for certain that anything you do is changing brain structure (unless you happen to have an MRI or PET scanner readily available in your classroom). Many of the activities suggested in so-called 'brain based learning' schemes will not do children any harm; at the very most they will waste some of your time in class that you might otherwise use delivering other aspects or types of instruction.

Summary

This chapter has looked at a range of psychological theories and schools of psychology related to learning, ranging from a behaviourist view of observable change to the social and culturally influenced theories of Feurstein and Vygotsky.

When this chapter was being planned, the first 'port of call' was the QTS standards. This proved to be an interesting exercise, since there were few direct references to the role of the teacher in promoting learning, and very little sense that pupil-learning is central to the process of teaching. This chapter has attempted to set learning at the heart of teaching, since it is our belief that if learning has not taken place, then neither has teaching. The theories and models set out in this chapter should provide a foundation for planning effective teaching that seeks to ensure that learning takes place. It is important that you know *why* and *how* children learn, not just what to do or what content to teach. This also means that you have a basis for reflection. As we will see in Chapter 10, being a reflective teacher is an important aspect of your professional development. An understanding of theories about learning will help your reflection to go beyond a superficial consideration of what works or does not work.

CHAPTER 5

The teacher and the community of the school

Introduction and chapter aims

A community is a group of people who interact with each other. Schools are changing their roles. Institutions which functioned between 9.00am and 3.30pm and which concentrated on delivering services predominantly in classrooms are extending to offer services between 8.00am and 6.00pm. The target is for half our schools to offer these wraparound services by 2008, with all being involved by 2010. This extended school initiative raises issues about the changing relationships between adults and children, and between adults and the school system, e.g. the different relationships in classrooms and breakfast clubs.

This chapter will:

- outline the functions of schools in communities;
- describe the biological bases of community;
- consider the role of culture in community;
- examine culture from different perspectives;
- describe some pitfalls in curriculum design;
- describe some processes found in human groups;
- present information about relationships in extended schools; and
- consider pupil motivation in the context of school culture.

Functions of schools

In one sense, schools have always been embedded in communities. Historically, however, the communities were small and quite specific. In England, schools were established in the fourteenth century near cathedrals. The names of our oldest schools may be familiar; Winchester and Shrewsbury, for example. They served the communities of church, government, diplomacy, law and administration by the teaching of Latin. The basis of these structures still drew on Roman principles and were written in Latin, the language of learning. The teachers had been pupils at these schools and had attended one of the two universities of the time, Oxford or Cambridge. So the function of schools was to provide suitably trained staff for these activities. The proportion of children receiving education was small and limited to the upper classes. It was not until the nineteenth century that education was seen to be a benefit to children from working-class families.

The industrial revolution led to families living in growing urban communities. Children worked in factories, but were free on Sundays. The church set up schools which taught basic literacy and numeracy on Sundays. So Sunday Schools were the first educational facilities for the masses. The *community* enlarged to cover most people. In 1870, the Education Act made provision of free education for children until ten years of age. In 1944, secondary education was established for all, up to the age of fifteen. This was increased to 16 in the 1970s. Although not a statute, successive governments have set increasingly higher targets for the number of young people staying in education beyond age sixteen. The community served by schools has increased to cover all living in the UK. Schools are now part of the British community and perform a range of functions including childcare; preparation for work; and teaching skills such as literacy, foreign languages, numeracy, life skills and technical competence. They provide opportunities for children to learn social skills, make friends and mix with large numbers of other people in the same age range. The educative function of schools may be similar to those fourteenth-century institutions, but the community which is served is very different. (For a more comprehensive history see Arnold and Yeomans 2005.) Within this context, we must consider the nature of community.

Biological bases of community

Humans are social animals. There are a few instances of children raised without human company and their development is markedly different and delayed. If we consider other primates we find similarity. They live in social groups, but of differing sizes. Research has considered the relationship between the size of brain and number of individuals living together in communities. While there is an aspect of group size determined by habitat, there appears to be an upper limit of social group for all primates. The hypothesis has been put that this limit exists due to cognitive constraints (Dunbar 1993). These constraints arise from cortical (brain) size and complexity and affect the number of relationships of which any individual can keep track.

Dunbar looked at cortical size and mean number of social links maintained by individuals for 36 different primate genera. There is a simple relationship. This can then be applied to humans to establish the maximum group size suggested by the size of our cortex. The result is found to be about 150. In other words, there is some evidence to suggest that we have a capacity to hold relationships with about 150 other people. In primate communities the formula is derived from the number of regular grooming partners and the limit of individuals who are willing to act as allies during conflicts. Time taken for social grooming increases in a more or less linear way with group size. As Dunbar points out, there is a need to balance the distance kept from other group members to protect access to food and reproductive opportunities with the need not to drive them away completely. An analogy in human terms is the maximum number of people we can know well enough to ask a favour of and reasonably expect it to be granted (ibid.). Clearly, this is highly specu-lative, but the theory is gathering support from a number of different sources. Most professional armies have units of about 150; in business, 150 is seen as a critical limit for effective co-ordination of tasks through direct person-to-person contact. Larger groups need sub-structures which define responsibility and communication (ibid.). Kilworth (1984) gave subjects descriptions of 500 different people. The descriptions were realistic, but fictional. The subjects were asked if they could identify people they knew who were similar to those described. The mean number was 134, surprisingly close to the 150 suggested by the cortical size hypothesis.

The implications for schools are interesting. Schools, typically, have populations which far exceed 150. Many secondary schools have populations in excess of 1,000, so if we are to consider schools as central to our communities, we may need to organise them into far smaller units. An eight-form entry secondary school may have 300 children each year. For a sense of identity to form, it may be necessary to create much smaller units, each with assigned staff and social opportunities.

Searle (1997) defined four principles of community:

- belongingness
- organisation
- unity
- struggle.

He readily acknowledges the context of his principles; a secondary school in Sheffield catering for children from many different heritages in an area of economic decline.

Calderwood (2000) expresses the importance of schools as part of a wider community:

> People believe in community. It is not only a cherished notion of close-knit humanity, but also a fundamental expression of the cooperative human social activity that ensures our survival as a species. Connection, caring, interdependence, shared values, rituals and celebrations, the security of being known, of belonging to a group, of being significant – these images, among many others, come to mind when one thinks of com-munity. Within our complex society, the social relations of community mitigate against anonymity and humanise our institution.

Community therefore, is seen as important for our well-being. Within communities there are cultures.

Culture and schools

Geertz (1968) defined culture as:

> an historically transmitted pattern of meaning embodied in symbols, a system of inherited conceptions expressed in symbolic form by means of which men communicate, perpetuate and develop their knowledge about and attitudes towards life.

Culture exists in families, communities, social groups, nations and, of course, schools.

The culture of a school can offer similarities to those of their client groups. It is, however, an important and sometimes disturbing idea that they may not be well aligned. An informal survey of teachers in their first year of service reveals that about half come from families with parents or other close relatives in teaching. The nature of the qualifications necessary for adults to become teachers is such that the majority of teachers were themselves successful at school. There is a tacit assumption that school is a good thing and is there to promote the best interests of the pupils. Children from backgrounds which have benefited from success in education will have been exposed to ideas about these benefits. Children from families for whom education was not a positive experience may have quite different ideas. So education exists in a cultural context. As an example of potential differences of culture having an impact on children in school we can consider the exclusion rates for boys from a black Afro-Caribbean heritage compared with other groups. It is justified to examine these differences through the differences in culture.

Ginwright (2004) has explored this theme in a school context. She starts by setting out different world views (Table 5.1):

Table 5.1 Afrocentric and western cultural world views compared

Afrocentric world-view	Western world-view
Self-knowledge is the basis of all knowledge. All is symbolic of spirit and manifesting.	*External knowledge* is the basis of all knowledge. One knows through counting and measuring.
Both/and mode of reasoning.	*Either/or* mode of reasoning.
Spirituality is the process by which goals will be achieved.	*Technology* is the most valued process by which goals will be reached.
Faith, choice, consciousness, belief are primary.	*Control* is the primary goal.
Choosing, acting and creating define power.	*Money, influence and politics* define power.
Happiness and peace define the purpose of life.	*Owning and possessing* define life's purpose.
Loves change and growth.	*Fears* change and internal growth.

While it is possible to challenge the depiction of the western world-view, the point still remains that there are *cultural* differences which may lead to higher rates of disaffection. Speaking about the educational system offered to African-American students, a lawyer commentated:

> We believe that the educational system created low self-esteem, low self-worth, and injures black students. Students are required to go to school by law, and yet it injures them because it promotes white culture, white civilisation, and it promotes supremacy . . . When you talk about giving a proper education and relevant education, you had to talk about African history, Afrocentric culture. For example, we had people looking at textbooks and we realised that black folks are not present in many textbooks.
>
> (ibid.)

Educational groupings can inadvertently communicate differences to children and contribute to a negative sense of self-worth. Within the national literacy and numeracy strategies found in the UK a number of schools use attainment based teaching groups. One school known to this author created a 'special needs' group which covered three school-year cohorts. The membership of this group was determined by low attainment in these curriculum areas and the school allocated more staff to assist the children. The group was composed predominantly of boys from an African-Caribbean heritage. Children from Year 6 (10/11-year-olds) were educated alongside children from Year 4 (7/8-year-olds). A clear message of inadequacy was communicated to the older children and a higher than expected degree of disaffection was found by the school, with children often being excluded for poor behaviour. The existence and membership of this group probably communicated a message not intended by the school.

Evidence of commonality across culture

When reviewing studies of education, communication and culture, the most favoured analysis examines differences. Culture is seen as something to describe, not comment on. There were studies which looked at differences in ability across cultures. Elsewhere, the work of Jensen is described. If there are differences in outcome for different cultures, extreme caution is exercised before drawing conclusions. So specifically cross-cultural *empirical* (or experimental) studies are not common; however, they can provide evidence of *commonality* between cultures. Competition has been studied empirically.

The use of competition as a motivational tool has been a feature of western education for a long time. The impact such a method might have in one eastern culture has been reported by Lam *et al.* (2004). They used a simple competitive situation in a mainstream Chinese school. The authors review the literature to find that the use of competition promotes performance goals at the expense of learning goals. While the performance of successful students may increase, that of less successful ones may decrease. Competition increases the pressure to seek positive evaluations and avoid negative ones. Students who are not under competitive pressure can develop competence and mastery. The differences are most noticeable if the students face a set-back or have low confidence. The performance-orientated students will avoid negative judgements of their work, while the learning-orientated ones will remain persistent and work towards mastery. They are not particularly concerned about comparison with other students' performances.

Motivation within competitive situations focuses on outperforming others; or the ability to win the subsequent self-evaluation of ability depends on performance compared with others. Ability is evaluated as high if the student wins, but low if they lose. Studies are cited which suggest that these students' performances may actually deteriorate after failure, whereas learning outcome-orientated students' performances do not. The authors comment on the cultural context of most of these studies. They are found in philosophically western-orientated environments. However, Chinese classes are known for their competitiveness and emphasis on examination success, but a competitive environment creates performance goals and unfavourable results for western classes. Paradoxically, the achievements of Chinese students are higher than those of western counterparts. Their study looked at Chinese students working in Hong Kong and created a paradigm in which students were taught Chinese typing for a short period. There were four groups; two were competitive and were told that their certificates would publish their relative positions at the end of the class, the other two were told that they would receive certificates of attendance. No mention was made of any position in class.

Students were given a computer-based teaching session followed by a test. They then had a second session followed by a second test. Students were asked to fill in a questionnaire which looked at:

- enjoyment of learning;
- attribution of test result; and
- self-efficacy on the next test.

The first teaching/testing cycle involved easy items, while the second used difficult ones. The students would generally succeed in the first, but experience failure in the second. Students could opt for an easy or more challenging test after the second tuition cycle. For a full description of the study it is necessary to consult the original. It is an intriguing study.

Findings were along the expected lines. The nature of the competitive/non-competitive situation created differences in outcome for the students. In particular:

- students in the competitive situation were more likely to opt for the easy test following failure in a previous test;
- students in the competitive situation had less self-efficacy and more negative self-evaluation than those in the non-competitive class; and

- students in the competitive class did better on the easy items than those in the non-competitive class, but slightly worse on the more difficult items.

They comment that competition acts as other externally controlling influences and gives students an 'external locus of causality for their learning'. Learning is no longer of intrinsic benefit to the student, rather a method of obtaining a positive external evaluation and avoiding a negative one.

The authors do discuss the limits of the study. A simple two-hour simulation cannot properly reflect processes taking place in classrooms over several years. However, there is reason to speculate that the competitive processes adopted in classrooms over time are actually detrimental to educational outcomes for the students. The authors suggest that this represents a challenge to those who suggest that cultural context represents an insurmountable barrier to education of students from different heritages.

Cultural bias in educational testing has been discussed for a long time and is explored in Chapter 9. The psychologist Jensen reported that children from an African-Caribbean heritage had lower IQ scores than their counterparts from white heritages. His work was heavily criticised for its racist findings. Others have attempted to circumvent the problem by distinguishing between the *technical* elements of tests from the *consequential* uses of tests. The technical elements focus on the needs of tests to satisfy questions of validity and freedom from social bias. The primary problem is to obtain accurate measurements, and the social setting of the use of the test is secondary. The consequentialists deny the sharp distinction between the test and the social setting. Questions of bias are seen as unavoidably embedded in social conditions. Educational testing practices must be evaluated in broad social terms. The outcomes of test use are of primary interest. Howe (1995) points out the flaws in this thinking. Any kind of performance testing occurs within a cultural context. The construction of the test will depend on the nature of the subject to be tested. The subject will always be embedded in culture.

The importance of language and verbal skills have been underlined recently by a longitudinal study examining the effects of various psycho-social variables on scholastic achievement and behaviour at school. Petrides *et al.* (2005) report that academic performance at the end of Key Stage 3 has a correlation of 0.92 with verbal skills. This reduces for GCSE results which have rather lower correlations (0.75 for boys and 0.92 for girls). The study also finds that absenteeism, truancy and exclusions are higher in pupils with poor verbal skills. The authors observe that pupils with poor verbal skills do not find it easy to meet course requirements, which alienate them from their educational environment. Some outgoing children will direct their interests to activities which are not conducive to educational attainment.

Insights from an experiential perspective

Some educational systems have experimented by changing the cultural basis of the school curriculum. Consider the initiative cited earlier by Ginwright (2004) who describes the Principles of Ma'at – an ancient Egyptian code of conduct or value system:

1. *Truth*: one must speak truth and do truth.

2. *Justice* is seen as a personal, social, economic, and political 'rightness' embedded in the balance between individual liberty and societal expectations.

3. *Righteousness* is seen as governing or relating, which is driven by the principle of reciprocity.

4. *Propriety* acknowledges that the most fundamental human desires are happiness and affection.

5. *Balance* refers to the state wherein all the elements are in equilibrium.

6. *Harmony* acknowledges the importance of order, balance, rhythm, and rapport for the sense of homeostasis.

7. *Order* is considered the first virtue because nothing is possible without order, including good.

(Ginwright 2004)

She describes how a curriculum was developed based on these principles. The biology curriculum is cited as an example (Table 5.2):

Table 5.2   The Ma'at principle shown through biological concepts (Ginwright 2004)

Week	Ma'at principle	Biological concepts
1	Truth	Learning about truth through scientific evidence and reason.
2	Balance	Understanding equilibrium and functions.
3	Harmony	Understanding transportation through cell wall and surrounding environment of the cell.
4	Order	Understanding basic cell structure.
5	Propriety	Understanding the proper function of a healthy cell (discuss viruses, cancer, steroids).
6	Justice	Understanding the proper environment for cells to grow.
7	Righteousness	Understanding how cells try to self-correct from an imbalance or outside influence.

The project went further in adopting Ebonics as the primary language of many African-American students, thus communicating with the pupils in the same language in which they spoke. This went as far as translating official documents into Ebonics and offering differentiated access to services for Ebonic-speaking students.

Overall, however, the project failed to meet its objectives. The new curriculum did not connect with students' concrete experiences and meaningful classroom practices. The students did not view the curriculum as relevant or meaningful to their daily lives. The author comments:

> While racial identity was certainly central to students at the school, many students viewed the project as an arrogant attempt to teach them how to be better at being black. The promotion of Egyptian culture throughout the project was celebrated at the expense of young people's unique economic struggles and their own hip-hop culture.

(Ginwright 2004)

The project was a bold experiment to improve the quality of education offered to pupils from a community with a long history of educational disadvantage, by communicating in the pupils' own language. The principles underpinning the innovation appeared to have a sound base, yet the application, ultimately, failed to change the outcomes for the targeted pupils. The author analysed the failure in terms of process. The project was led by adults and did not engage with the students themselves. She suggests five guiding principles for the promotion of reform:

1   Students are taught to analyse power within social relationships. This includes understanding the misuse of power in institutions as well as critical thinking about racism, sexism, homophobia and other forms of oppression.

2   Students connect ethnic identity development to broader issues of racial and economic justice. Inequality can be linked to identity. If students experience similar forms of social inequality they can work together to challenge it.

3   Students learn how to promote systemic change. Institutional practices that do not meet students' needs need to be challenged.

4   Students act through collective organising. The capacity to change oppressive social conditions lies in collective efforts, not just individual ones.

5   Adults embrace youth culture. Social justice is high on the agenda for change in most youth groups.

THEORY AND PRACTICE LINKS

Culture, beliefs and practices in classes

Consider the different cultural groups that you teach. What elements of difference do they have from your culture? What beliefs do you hold about their culture and practices? How might your interactions with the students be interpreted differently?

For example, pupils from families with poor literacy may not value learning to read in the same way that other pupils do. Pupils may not have the same opportunity to practise reading at home.

The Ginwright study is a cautionary tale for those who aspire to social engineering through education, but there is at least one additional element to be considered.

Woolfson *et al.* (2004) surveyed a primary school which had nearly 10 per cent of pupils from mainly Asian heritages. They used qualitative methods including questionnaires, semi-structured interviews and focus groups. Pupils, teachers, support staff and parents/carers were included in the study. The results suggested a high degree of agreement that discrimination on racial grounds was not evident and that the school had effective policies to prevent racism and bullying. Yet pupils from both the ethnic minority and white majority experienced racism and were still reluctant to disclose these experiences to staff. The authors describe the dangers of assuming a 'no problem here' stance, even in a school with well-established policies.

THEORY AND PRACTICE LINK

Culture and parents' evenings

Application: Consider a parents' evening. What expectations do you have regarding their attendance? What differences in attribution do you make about parents from different groups?

Processes in groups

Within communities there are varieties of groups of people. Studies of the types of groups found in animal communities offer the following possibilities:

1 *Solitary animals* – adults live separate lives and only meet in the breeding season. Examples of mammals include bears, pandas and raccoons.

2 *Pairs* – some mammals such as beavers, jackals, foxes and gibbons pair-bond, but most mammals do not. The females tend to care for the young without male assistance.

3 *Family* – this is an extension of the pair. When young are born, they are raised by both parents until such time as the parents have another litter or they are driven away to form their own pairs.

4 *Harem* – one dominant male mates with a number of different females. Some harems are permanent, e.g. patas monkey; others, like the red deer, exist only in the breeding season.

5 *Matriarchy* – a harem can convert to a matriarchy when the females stay together at the centre of the group, with the males becoming peripheral. The males are given access to the females for breeding. Elephants are an example of this system.

6 *Oligarchy* – power is found in a small group of dominant males. Females mate with a number of these powerful males. Young males are driven out of the group. A 'pecking order' can develop among the males, with dominant males having more opportunities for mating. Wolves and common baboons operate in this way.

7 *Arena* – all males group together in the breeding season and display to attract a mate. The females visit the group, or arena to select a male.

8 *Hierarchy* – individuals are ranked according to status. High-ranking individuals displace lower ones in choice of feeding place and mate.

9 *Aggregation* – non-breeding groups can grow in size, particularly in migrations. This has the advantage of offering protection from predators. Antelopes and many birds display this grouping.

10 *Caste system* – different individuals perform different tasks. Bees, ants and termites become workers, drones, soldiers and contribute to the running of large communities of the species.

(adapted from Morris 1990)

The biological origins of our communities, therefore, may be surprisingly complex. Human groups have been extensively studied. A well-used analysis of human group development has been described by Tuckman and Jensen (1977). They describe five *stages* in the development of a human group and use the terms forming, storming, norming, performing and adjourning to describe them.

1 *Forming.* When groups of people first meet together, there is a dependence on previous ways of interacting. People form impressions of others. The social rules are to keep things simple. There is uncertainty about the purpose of the group and dependence on any identifiable leaders. The individuals seek orientation of function.

2 *Storming.* Individuals start to conflict and compete for different roles, including leadership. The discomfort can lead to some individuals remaining silent, while others appear aggressive.

3 *Norming.* When the majority of the roles have been, at least provisionally, agreed, the group members begin to co-operate and collaborate. Members listen to each other and become willing to accept the views of other group members. The type of language used becomes agreed. There is a general sense of the group cohesion.

4 *Performing.* The group members become interdependent. The roles are well understood and the tasks are achieved efficiently and collaboratively.

5 *Adjourning.* At the end of the life of the group, the members begin to disengage. There is sadness. People recall the good times; 'Wasn't it good when we . . .'.

The nature of these processes may reflect social processes in biologically less complex species. The storming phase may be linked to the establishment of pecking orders in hierarchically organised societies. Performing suggests an agreement of complementary roles, perhaps akin to a caste community.

We can apply these processes to classrooms with new social groupings, including teachers. An initial 'honeymoon' period is followed by challenges from children testing boundaries before establishing some stability. In secondary schools, classrooms may be *arenas* for adolescents to display. Anger in children in a classroom can reflect defence or display (Arnold and Yeomans 2005). Both may have biological origins.

Within the groups found in schools the roles that teachers are required to play vary. They include:

- leadership;
- pupil management;
- support staff management;
- managing learning;
- managing resources;
- assessing outcomes;
- maintaining relationships; and
- mediating individual relationships.

There are many more. Each new group may need to progress through the stages described in order to be productive. The primary focus for teachers has concentrated on learning in classrooms. Outcomes have been measured in terms of standards of academic achievement. The educational agenda is changing. Schools of the future will offer wider varieties of services.

Extended school days

There are moves to change the nature of schools in the community. *Extended* schools will provide services from 8.00 am to at least 6.00 pm in order to facilitate the needs of parents who work. The government's targets are that 50 per cent of schools will offer wraparound services by 2008 and all will do so by 2010. Breakfast clubs and after-school activities are becoming more widely available. These initiatives bring new and sometimes challenging roles to the adults who work in them. Consider the domestic nature of most homes and contrast this with a typical classroom (see Table 5.3).

We can create a dimension with home and classrooms being contrasting environments. The extent to which breakfast and out-of-school clubs are similar to either home or classrooms may become important in shaping the experiences of the next generation of children to pass through our educational systems.

Table 5.3 Homes and classrooms compared

Home	Classroom
Small number of children per adult.	Large numbers of children per adult.
Personal and private space.	Public space.
Choice of where to go in the house.	Adults direct where children go in the classroom/school.
Choice of what to wear.	Institutional determination of clothes.
Informal time allocation, timetables unusual.	Formal allocation of time and timetable.
Informal system of rules.	Formal use of rules/rewards/corrections.
Physical intimacy permitted.	Physical intimacy prohibited.
Choice of activities, including doing nothing.	Adult direction of activities. Doing nothing usually discouraged.
No particular work emphasis.	Emphasis on curriculum-based work.

In a small-scale study conducted in a community school with established breakfast and after-school clubs, children were asked to indicate the similarities and differences between home, classrooms and the clubs. Where there were similarities between two of these they were picked out. Additionally, if items were different or the same in all three places they were coded accordingly. We express the results in two ways:

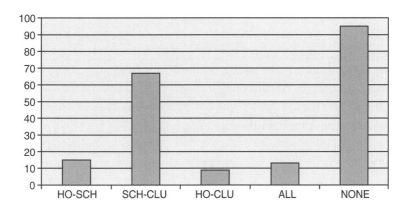

Key:
HO – home; SCH – school classroom; CLU – club
ALL: The items were mentioned as occurring at home, school classroom and club.
NONE: The items were mentioned as occurring in only one of the environments.

Figure 5.1 Home/school/club similarities – Junior School (Merriman and Arnold 2006)

The conclusions are clear; while many of the features were unique, the clubs had much greater similarity to the classroom than the home. We can visualise the individual elements in a Venn diagram:

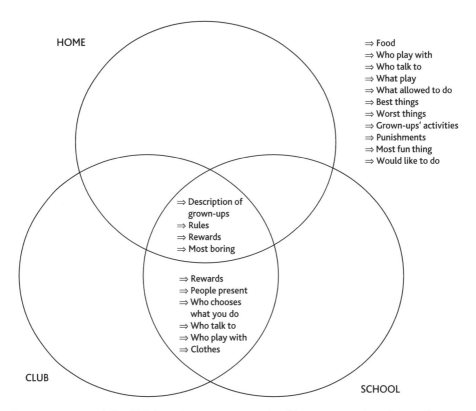

Figure 5.2 Home/school/club similarities – Junior School (Merriman and Arnold 2006)

So it would seem that the experience of the extended day is akin to an extended school day rather than school taking on the less formal attributes of a domestic environment. The adults running the after-school clubs showed awareness of the issue. One said that the children come out of school as 'high as kites' and need to 'let off steam', at least for a while. The club, however, is organised with assigned groups and timetabled activities. Cohen and Manion (1989) observed: 'Rituals and routines are invaluable to the teacher for, in imposing a structure on the life of the school, they offer . . . a base for establishing control, thereby prolonging . . . survival chances day by day, year by year'.

Many children arriving at home may simply watch television and relax. This appears to be a less favoured option in after-school clubs. One head teacher commented that if she was responsible for the running of the club, her first priority was safety. We rely on structure to promote order. The staff use existing skills of rules and routines to create that structure.

The extension of services offered by schools may develop into a prolonging of time spent in institutions regulated by rules and routines. We discussed briefly the contribution of Bowlby in Chapter 1. His work warns against the increase in institutional care of children. Although this may seem an extreme generalisation of work conducted over 50 years ago, it suggests a need for great care and evaluation of this project. The impact of providing more opportunities for adults to work needs to be set against the need to create longer school days.

Evaluating such initiatives creates needs for new paradigms. Simple cause–process–effect analyses which ignore the context usually miss important information. Pawson and Tilley (1997) provide a model which may be helpful. They describe eight rules:

1 Evaluators need to attend to how and why social programmes have the potential to cause change.

2 Evaluators need to penetrate beneath the surface of observable inputs and outputs of a programme.

3 Evaluators need to focus on how the causal mechanisms which generate social and behavioural problems are removed or countered through the alternative causal mechanisms introduced in a social programme.

4 Evaluators need to understand the contexts within which problem mechanisms are activated and in which programme mechanisms can be successfully fired.

5 Evaluators need to understand what are the outcomes of an initiative and how they are produced.

6 In order to develop transferable and cumulative lessons from research, evaluators need to orient their thinking to context–mechanism–outcome pattern configurations.

7 In order to achieve point 6, evaluators need to engage in a teacher–learner relationship with programme policy makers, practitioners and participants.

8 Evaluators need to acknowledge that programmes are implemented in a changing and permeable world and that programme effectiveness may thus be subverted or enhanced through the unanticipated intrusion of new contexts and new causal powers.

A comprehensive evaluation needs to be undertaken if we are to improve the lives of large numbers of children. Encouraging parents to work and use the extended schools' new facilities may seem attractive; however, the point remains that if schools are going to offer extended services to the community, the nature of the relationship between the adults and children needs to be reconsidered if we are to avoid creating increasingly institutionalised children. Teachers may be placed under pressure to produce more homework to occupy children between

3.30 pm and 6.00 pm. Children may spend 50 hours per week in these extended schools. We must remember that a directive from the European Parliament limits an adult's working week to 48 hours. There is a danger that we are creating working environments for children with demands that exceed those for adults. While there is a place for children to learn and practise working independently, a balance needs to be struck if schools are to take larger parts of a child's waking experience.

Motivation and community

The different functions of schools in communities lead to differences in motivation for pupils. We present three approaches to motivation in schools:

- biological
- behavioural
- cognitive.

Biological

This school emphasises the role of goals. Humans have needs and our actions are designed to get these needs met. Maslow suggested that our needs can be arranged hierarchically (see Figure 5.3). Children may work to achieve the possibility of a better-paid job and more opportunities for pleasure or social status. If schools are perceived as helping pupils attain these goals, the pupils are more likely to collaborate with the work assigned.

A practical application of this was found in a comprehensive school in a part of the West Midlands with higher-than-average unemployment. The school surveyed local employers and asked what they would want pupils from the school to be able to do for them in order to be employed by the firm. The findings formed the basis of a vocational curriculum in Key Stage 4. This had considerable influence on pupils who traditionally became disaffected by school.

Behavioural

This approach highlights the consequences of particular actions. People behave because they associate rewards with these actions. They repeat the behaviour to gain further rewards. (It is also the case that people avoid actions which lead to negative consequences.) Schools which systematically reward good work or behaviour are likely to create communities in which good work and behaviour are found and valued.

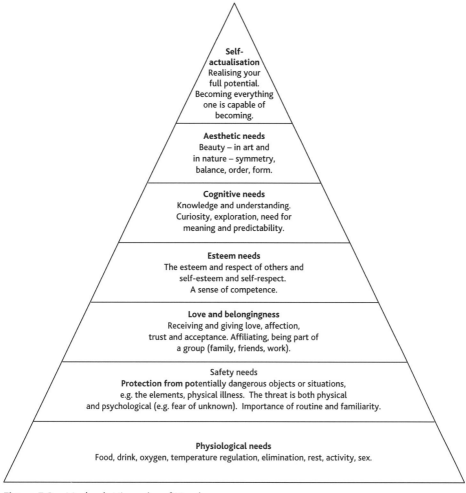

Figure 5.3 Maslow's Hierarchy of Needs

There are two elements of particular importance:

- contingency – the reward must only be given if the action has occurred; and
- contiguity – the link between the action and the reward must be clear to the pupil.

Schools have incentive schemes. Children are rewarded with stickers saying 'Well done' or 'Good work'. Star charts in classes are commonplace. Some teachers send positive letters home. Rewards do not need to be tangible; a smile or simple social praise are probably the most commonly used rewards.

Some criticism of incentive-based schemes has been voiced. Kohn (1999) suggests that rewards are based on an unequal distribution of power. The person giving the reward uses it to control the child. The need of the adult to control may determine what is rewarded. This may not be in the child's best interests. Furthermore, the use of rewards (particularly tangible ones) suggests that there may be more value in the reward itself than in the action which is being rewarded. A child rewarded by being excused homework might reasonably conclude that the homework itself has little value. Kohn cites an example of a dieting study. Subjects were promised a five-dollar reward twice a week if they lost weight. These subjects did lose more weight than the other (unrewarded) group; however, they put the weight back on when the rewards stopped. By contrast, the unrewarded group continued to lose weight.

In spite of these reservations, most schools do use incentive schemes. For young children, the perception of the value of school work may not be well formed. Rewards-based schools tend to have better behaviour and academic results than those that are not.

Cognitive

Entwistle and Kozeki (1985) described links between approaches to and styles of learning with different motivations. They outlined three successful orientations and one unsuccessful one:

Orientation 1: *Meaning*. Pupils look for a deep understanding of the subject in a holistic way. Their motivation is intrinsic. They believe that school helps them to do well.

Orientation 2: *Reproducing*. Pupils only look at the surface of the work. They reproduce work by memorising it rather than analysing it. Their main motivation is the avoidance of failure or need to please significant adults. They work for the qualification rather than any intrinsic value in the work.

Orientation 3: *Achieving*; Pupils analyse what is needed to get good marks. They are conscientious, working long hours to get the work right. They are motivated by a hope for success.

Orientation 4: *Non-academic*. Pupils do not see the value of studying.

There are questionnaires available to elicit the pupil's approach to learning.

Analysing the views of pupils can only serve to enhance the links between schools and the communities they serve. Whether this is done by questionnaire, school council or regular discussion is less important than the elicitation itself. Untested assumptions about the motives of pupils from different communities can lead to costly mistakes (e.g. Ginwright 2004). What motivates children in one area may be very different from that which motivates children in a different place. Communities differ, and schools need to reflect these differences.

Summary

This chapter has considered schools both as embedded in communities and as communities in themselves. It has suggested that differences in communities need to be taken into account when planning activities in schools. A 'one size fits all' approach to selecting a curriculum may not be particularly successful. The dangers of centralising the curriculum are clear. Cultural differences can be reflected in different pupil motivation. Schools are probably in the best place to determine what the priorities are for the local communities and may feel trapped into delivering material that is not well suited to their client group. As schools develop their roles by offering extended services, they need to be sensitive to the different needs of the communities they serve.

CHAPTER 6

Managing the classroom

Introduction and chapter aims

> Our earth is degenerate in these latter days; bribery and corruption are common; children no longer obey their parents and the end of the world is evidently approaching.

> (Assyrian clay tablet, 2800 BC)

Although the wording is not particularly twenty-first century, the sentiments certainly are. These opinions would not be out of place in many newspapers or school staffrooms. Concerns about the behaviour of children and young people are nothing new. Twenty years after the publication of the Elton Report on discipline in schools, a government task force has been appointed to investigate pupil behaviour once again.

Managing your classroom effectively is probably one of the most difficult tasks involved in teaching. An ill-disciplined or unruly class affects both pupils and teachers: pupils do not learn and teachers become stressed. The consequences of poor pupil discipline are enormous; for example, poor examination results, difficult relationships with the local community, staff absence due to work-related stress and problems with recruitment and retention of staff.

This chapter aims to examine different models of classroom management, and in doing so will draw on a number of psychological theories. Theory and practice links will be made in order to help you to apply chapter content to your classroom, with the aim that you will be able to enhance your classroom management. The chapter will first look at a range of psychological perspectives in relation to classroom management. It will then look at the way in which these perspectives can be applied in the classroom, by suggesting a model of theory application that we call the 'root and branch' model.

Psychological perspectives on classroom behaviour management

The behavioural perspective

The behavioural perspective is probably the most widely used application of psychology in relation to classroom management. There are four key principles in this perspective:

1 Behaviour is learned;

2 behaviour can change;

3 behaviour is affected by antecedents; and

4 behaviour is affected by consequences.

Behaviour is learned

One of the defining characteristics of a behavioural perspective is its rejection of the role of nature in shaping individuals and their behaviour. Therefore, the behaviour of your pupils is not due to fixed personality traits or their genes, but is something that has been learned over time. The environmental conditions that they have been exposed to will have shaped their behaviour for good or ill. These conditions relate to antecedents and consequences, which will be examined later. Learned behaviour relates to your role as a teacher. One of the myths about teaching that the Elton Report described is: 'Teachers are born, not made'. While there might be some genetic predispositions (although a strict behavioural perspective would reject the notion of predisposition) it is possible to learn the skills involved in managing classroom behaviour. An example of this learning on the part of teachers can be found in the Assertive Discipline Programme (Canter and Canter 1992). A key concept in this programme is that teachers should be assertive in demanding appropriate classroom behaviour and that teachers can learn to be assertive. The programme goes on to teach the skills of assertiveness as a foundation for implementing a range of classroom management strategies.

Behaviour can change

This key principle follows on from the first. If we believe that behaviour is learned then we have to also believe that behaviour can change; that is, we can learn new and different behaviours. Therefore, when you are faced with a difficult or unruly class, keep in mind that if they have learned how to behave in this way; therefore it is perfectly possible for them to learn to behave in a more acceptable way. This premise, in turn, suggests that teaching needs to take place. You cannot simply expect that all your pupils will *know* how to behave. As teachers it is important that you take responsibility for teaching appropriate behaviour to your pupils; this is what effective classroom management is about.

Behaviour is affected by antecedents

Antecedents are the things that lead up to behaviour, or the contexts for behaviour. Changes in antecedents can produce changes in behaviour. There are two types of antecedents: environmental antecedents and setting events.

Environmental antecedents relate to the impact of the physical environment. This would include the effect of heating and lighting in a classroom. Sometimes it is not possible to change these. However, there are other aspects of the classroom environment that *are* under your control. For example, you can have some control over seating arrangements and location of resources. Research carried out by Wheldall and Lam (1987) showed that levels of on-task behaviour in primary classrooms increased when pupils were seated in rows rather than in table groups.

Setting events relate to other contexts for behaviour that are not specifically linked to the physical environment. On a very general level, a setting event would relate to *where* you are. For example, you and your colleagues would behave at an INSET meeting differently from how you would act at the pub afterwards. You are the same people, but the setting in which you are placed affects your behaviour. The same is true of pupils. Behaviour on a playing field will be different from behaviour in assembly.

Two important setting events are crucial aspects of effective behaviour management: rules and directions. Both set the context for behaviour by stating what is expected.

A *rule* is something that applies all the time. For example, 'keep left when going down stairs' will apply at all times in school. There are a number of criteria for effective rules, as follows:

- Wherever possible, they should be observable. If your rules are ambiguous (for example, 'Be sensible') then you will not be able to establish the precise behaviours you want to see. Furthermore, you risk being sucked into arguments with pupils about their interpretation of the rule ('But I was being sensible'). If you cannot be precise, then make sure you generate a list of examples of observable behaviours that would indicate that the rule is being followed. For example, many schools have rules about respect. Make sure your pupils know what behaviours would indicate that they are showing respect.

- They should be positive. If your rule tells pupils how to behave (rather than how *not* to behave) then it is much easier to recognise and reinforce desired behaviour.

- Only have a rule for a behaviour that you need to address.

- Only use a small number of rules (three or four for Key Stages 1 and 2, maximum of five for key stages 3 and 4). If you use any more, both you and your pupils will not remember them. It will be difficult to recognise and reinforce behaviour that relates to a list of ten rules (even if they are positive).

Rules can fall into four main groups:

- relations with adults and peers ('speak politely');
- academic work ('hand in homework on time');
- classroom routines ('line up quietly'); and
- safety ('walk in the corridors').

If your pupils are behaving inappropriately, one of the first things to consider is whether you have given them clear expectations. Do your pupils know what you expect them to do? The activity below is designed to help you generate some rules for your classroom.

Application assignment: generating rules

Fill in the table below. Start by listing some of the undesirable behaviours that your pupils engage in. Then, in the next column, write down an alternative, desirable behaviour. It should be incompatible with the undesirable behaviour. Two examples have been done for you.

Remember to make sure that the desirable behaviour is expressed positively and is an observable behaviour wherever possible.

Table 6.1   Fair pairs of children's behaviour

Undesirable behaviour	Desirable behaviour
Throwing objects	Keep objects to yourself
Shouting out in class discussions	Wait your turn

When you have completed the table, choose two or three behaviours from the right-hand column. These will form the basis of your classroom rules.

Complete the following table:

My classroom rules are:

I will communicate these rules to my pupils in the following ways:

Date to review these rules:

A *direction* applies to specific circumstances or contexts. It can be viewed as a temporary rule. An example might be in relation to the need for silence. In some lessons or activities, silence will be an important requirement. However, we would not want to have a rule expecting pupils to be silent that applied all the time.

There are specific activities that might require you to generate a set of directions that would only apply to that activity. For example, you might have a set of directions for behaviour in PE lessons that would only apply to these lessons. There are four main types of activity that might require directions:

- introducing a new activity to a class, such as going swimming for the first time;
- an activity that has a history of difficulty; for example, an activity that involves movement around or outside school might be something that has been fraught with problems due to inappropriate behaviour;
- activities that have health and safety implications, such as using a particular machine or piece of equipment in a design and technology lesson; and
- activities that are complex; this relates to activities that have a number of steps involved; for example, in a science experiment.

Behaviour is affected by consequences

One of the fundamental tenets of a behavioural perspective is that behaviour is shaped by its consequences. We stated earlier that behaviour can change. The way in which this behaviour change is effected is via reinforcement. Behaviour change will also be affected by the level and type of reinforcement. A behavioural perspective states that behaviour is more likely to be repeated if the consequences are pleasant; that is, if reinforcement is positive. We would stop engaging in a particular behaviour if the consequences are negative. In both cases, the behaviour has been affected by its consequences.

Rewards and punishments are part of a process of delivering or withholding reinforcement. A reward involves the delivery of a positive consequence (or, conversely, could involve withholding a negative consequence). Punishment involves delivering a negative consequence. It can also involve removing privileges (this is called response cost). The issue of rewards and punishment can be very complex if we do not think through its effects. The following gives an example of this complexity.

REWARDS AND PUNISHMENTS: WHAT'S THE PAY OFF?

A behavioural perspective states that behaviour is more likely to be repeated when it is followed by positive reinforcement.

The scenarios below both contain positive reinforcement; but are the outcomes what the teacher wants?

SCENARIO 1

Edward is a real nuisance in class. He's out of his seat several times during a lesson and rarely finishes any work. His teacher would be very pleased if he stayed in his seat and completed his work. Whenever he is out of his seat, his teacher says 'Edward sit down'. Whenever he is in his seat his teacher ignores him. She complains; 'I keep telling him to sit down but he still keeps on getting out of his seat. Why can't he learn how to get on with his work?'.

The problem here is that Edward's teacher is positively reinforcing the inappropriate behaviour. What Edward has learned is that his teacher only pays attention to him when he is out of his seat. When he does do what she wants, he is ignored and receives no positive reinforcement.

SCENARIO 2

Harry is in Year 1 and has some language and communication problems. His understanding of language is poor and he has problems making himself understood.

He finds it difficult to gain the teacher's attention sometimes, so he has found a way that is guaranteed to make her take notice of him: he wipes his nose on her skirt. When this happens, his teacher says very sarcastically; 'Thank you very much'. Then she gets cross with him. The nose-wiping behaviour doesn't go away. Harry's teacher complains: 'I always tell him off when he does it and it has no effect at all. If his language is that poor perhaps he should go to a special school. We can't have that sort of behaviour here'.

*The problem is that the teacher's response is positively reinforcing Harry's behaviour. He does not understand sarcasm (many young children do not, **and** Harry has some language difficulties). So when his teacher says 'Thank you very much', he takes it at face value and thinks she likes him to wipe his nose on her skirt.*

The message from these scenarios is that you must think carefully when giving consequences. In all the scenarios the teacher thought that they were giving an appropriate consequence to the pupil's behaviour when, in fact, they were not. What was construed as a reward or a punishment was exactly the opposite as far as the pupil was concerned. The most worrying aspect is that in the second of these scenarios the teacher had decided that the pupil should not be educated in a mainstream school. Although the scenarios are fictitious, they are based on real-life examples experienced by the authors, so the issues of school placement and labelling as a result of an erroneous approach to pupil management are quite real.

Having looked at some of the problems that might arise as a result of misuse of consequences, it is important now to identify what should be considered in order to ensure that the consequences we apply to behaviour are effective. The following gives some essential points about the use of reinforcement in the classroom, together with an application activity.

THEORY AND PRACTICE LINKS

Use of reinforcement in the classroom – effective rewards

In order to ensure that desirable behaviour is repeated, it should always be followed by a positive consequence. Therefore, rewarding pupils is an important part of teaching behaviour change. Effective rewards can be things that you say or do. You do not always have to give concrete objects. If you think back to the earlier scenarios, teacher attention to the right behaviour would have resulted in a change. Praise is something that you can give at any time and it doesn't cost anything. Some pupils will do anything for teacher attention, so if that is the case, use it. Doing jobs or having short amounts of individual time with the teacher can be effective. Sometimes just a smile or gesture in the direction of the pupil is enough to tell them that you have noticed their good behaviour.

Many schools have rewards that are used on a whole-school basis. If your school has a behaviour or discipline plan, it is important that you follow it. You might feel that you want to use your own class-wide rewards in addition to what happens in the school as a whole. For example, if the school-based rewards take the form of house points, you could add your own rewards when a set target of points is achieved. If you are planning behaviour management strategies to use with your class or teaching groups, take note of the following when you are planning what to do.

Effective rewards should:

- be valued by pupils;
- be in proportion to the behaviour (this means that you don't offer a huge reward for a relatively small behaviour change);
- be faded out gradually as behaviour change is established and maintained;
- be age-appropriate;
- show variety: reward can take the form of gestures, words and delivery of stars, tokens or objects; and
- be used in a 3:1 ratio to reprimands or sanctions (that is, three times more rewards than sanctions).

APPLICATION ACTIVITY

Now think about the class or classes that you teach. Write down the kind of rewards you can use. If you are not sure what they value, try asking the pupils, or draw up a 'menu' from which they can choose.

THEORY AND PRACTICE LINKS

Use of reinforcement in the classroom – effective sanctions

In order to ensure that undesirable behaviour is not repeated, it should always be followed by a negative consequence. Therefore, sanctions are an important part of teaching behaviour change.

Many schools have sanctions that are used on a whole-school basis. If your school has a behaviour or discipline plan it is important that you follow it. However, responses to undesirable behaviour can be planned that will not conflict with any school-wide sanctions. These are suggested as follows:

Positive reprimand

A positive reprimand describes the undesirable behaviour but also describes the desired behaviour. Here is an example:

> 'David, pushing in the line breaks our rule about keeping your hands to yourself. I want you to join the end of the line and keep your hands to yourself.'

As soon as David joins the line without pushing, praise this behaviour.

Separation

There are various types of separation. The easiest is to move the pupil away from others in the class. Do this for a set period of time (maximum of five minutes) then allow the pupil back to his or her usual seat. Praise the pupil as soon as s/he behaves appropriately after returning. Separation can also involve moving to another class or being sent to a senior member of staff. If you use this form of separation, make sure that you have an agreement with staff involved and always provide work.

Removal of privileges

This type of sanction means taking away time from a favoured activity. Often this takes the form of missing part of break time. If you use this sanction, do not keep the pupil in for the whole of break time; allow time for the pupil to go and have a break and let off steam and for you to have a break too. Do not use the curriculum with this type of sanction. For example, many pupils enjoy PE, but denying access to this as a sanction is not appropriate as the pupil is being denied his or her curriculum entitlement.

Effective sanctions should:

- be something that the pupil does not like or will avoid;
- never be humiliating or physical;
- be used in the context of the 3:1 praise and reprimand ratio (that means that whenever you use a sanction you must find three opportunities to praise the pupil);
- be arranged in a hierarchy, so that the pupil gradually moves through increasingly severe consequences (for example: warning; lose two minutes of break; lose five minutes of break; go to another class; go to the head or deputy);
- be preceded by a warning (but only one: do not constantly threaten or give 'last warnings' without following them through); and
- be in proportion to the behaviour (do not go 'over the top' and use the most severe sanction available for relatively minor misbehaviour).

APPLICATION ACTIVITY

Now think of some sanctions that you could use in your classroom. Arrange them in a hierarchy, so that you start with a warning and then progress through increasingly severe sanctions. If you are using these in your classroom, make sure that you can carry them out, i.e. do not put separation to another class on your list if you do not have an agreement with another member of staff.

Applications of the behavioural perspective

Key elements of a behavioural approach are the relationships between the setting (or antecedents), behaviour and events following the behaviour (consequences). There have been many studies focusing on the actions of teachers and the outcomes for children. A common framework looks at teacher responses to pupils (in terms of positive and negative comments made in response to academic and social behaviour; these can be expressed as AC+, AC–, SOC+ and SOC–) and pupil on-task behaviour.

Wheldall *et al.* (1987 and 1989) found ratios of about 3 : 1 for positive and negative academic praise and about 1 : 3 for positive and negative social praise. This meant that teachers were about three times more likely to praise children's work than criticise it, and about three times more likely to criticise children's behaviour than praise it. Similar findings were reported more recently by Harrop and Swinson (2000), with ratios for academic responses very similar to those found by Wheldall and Merrett, but with ratios of between 1 : 10 and 1 : 15 for positive and negative social responses.

Surprisingly little has been published examining the impact of *changing* teaching styles and analysing the impact using behavioural methods. However, work has been done with some very interesting results. Consider the work of Story (2005).

Story has developed a classification of teaching which divides teacher/student activities into four categories:

Table 6.2   Story's categories of teaching taxonomy

Lecture/demonstration	The teacher lectures/demonstrates to the class and the students sit and listen/watch.
Interactive teaching	There is an active interchange between the teacher and the class, in its simplest form 'question and answer'.
Individual student work	Students work individually on tasks set by the teacher.
Pair/group work	Students work in pairs or in groups on tasks set by the teacher.

Other measures included the nature of teacher comments to students (Ac+, Ac–, Soc+, Soc–). The critical measure is time on task, this being perhaps the most significant factor in assessing classroom behaviour and learning.

Findings from an action research project conducted in a secondary school which had requested an intervention with behaviour and learning included:

1   A high correlation ($r = 0.768$ statistically significant at $p<0.01$) between time on task and the ratio of academic comments, positive:negative. So a more positive orientation in academic comments by the teacher was associated with higher levels of on-task in students.

2   A similar, but lesser, effect was found in relation to the social praise to correction ratio. The correlation is 0.552 (statistically significant at $p<0.05$).

3   The level of interactive teaching and student on-task time was also highly correlated (0.81 statistically significant at $p<0.01$).

4. When teachers increased and combined their use of interactive teaching and the positive orientation of their comments it seemed to increase time on task. Furthermore, the increases were significantly greater for those classes that initially had low on-task levels. The correlation was −0.952 (statistically significant at $p<0.001$). (Those classes with initially low on-task levels had the greatest possibility of significantly increasing them.) If findings 1, 2 and 3 are combined, the teachers of those classes also had the greatest opportunity to increase the positive orientation of their comments and increase levels of interactive teaching.

Story (ibid.) has achieved similar results in many other secondary departments, but they have not been subject to the same rigorous statistical analysis.

One application of this work is to suggest practical strategies for improving the work of students. Increases in the positive orientation of teacher comments alongside interactive teaching are associated with increased time on task.

This work demonstrates the successful application of behavioural approaches to classrooms; however, we have not described the *processes* of change.

The behavioural perspective: summary and consideration of advantages and disadvantages

This section has given an overview of the way in which a behavioural perspective can be used in classroom management. It forms the most substantial section of this chapter as it is the most commonly used theory in behaviour management. This approach to classroom management relies on making changes to both antecedents and consequences in order to bring about changes in behaviour. Since the application of a behavioural perspective is very prevalent in approaches to classroom management, it is important to consider its advantages and disadvantages.

The main advantages of use of a behavioural perspective are:

- the techniques are easy for class teachers to adopt in their own classroom setting, without having to try to make major changes to the school system;

- the techniques can help to effect *rapid control* over difficult classroom behaviour, particularly when a class or group is exhibiting undesirable behaviour;

- strategies used can be explained easily to pupils, in terms of cause and effect (if you do X then Y will happen); and

- the approaches are backed up by a large body of evidence concerning their effectiveness.

The main disadvantages of use of a behavioural perspective are suggested as follows:

- the approaches can be seen as very 'teacher directed' and therefore undemocratic in terms of pupil involvement;
- there is little or no consideration given to feelings or emotions;
- the approaches can be viewed as being very isolated from the school as a whole, with little regard for the impact of wider systems on pupil behaviour (although this argument can be countered by the fact that a behavioural perspective does acknowledge the role of antecedents); and
- there is little or no emphasis on teacher and pupil relationships: the approaches can be viewed as a rather mechanistic delivery of consequences. One of the identified difficulties inherent in applying a behavioural perspective is that consequence management is over-emphasised at the expense of consideration of antecedents.

Despite these disadvantages, it is our contention that use of techniques and strategies derived from behavioural psychology is straightforward, easy to implement and effective. Many of the other approaches that this chapter will consider will require a great deal more teacher effort in order to implement them successfully. Furthermore, the advantage of rapid control is crucial. If you are faced with a disruptive and unruly group or class, your priority is to establish firm and effective discipline that creates a calm and ordered classroom where teaching and learning can take place. You might find that establishing rapid and effective control then gives you the freedom to use other psychological models that address some of the disadvantages of the behavioural perspective. We now consider the application of other psychological models.

The psychodynamic perspective

The psychodynamic perspective is derived from the work of Sigmund Freud. The emphasis in this approach is on feelings and emotions, with introspection and self-awareness being important aspects of the theory in action. Since Freud's original work, the psychodynamic 'stable' has expanded considerably. The examples discussed in the next two sections are not strictly Freudian. In both cases the psychologists responsible for generating the original ideas began their professional careers within the Freudian 'stable', but in both cases moved on from Freud's perspective. Nevertheless, both approaches remain within a psychodynamic perspective due to their basic emphasis on feelings, emotions and self-awareness.

Transactional Analysis

Transactional Analysis (TA) was developed by Eric Berne (1910–70). Berne trained as a psychotherapist and worked with Eric Erikson (see Chapter 2 for a full account of Erikson's theory about human development). Berne challenged the Freudian idea of the unconscious, focusing on studies of intuition. He was prompted to develop a new psychotherapeutic approach after being rejected for membership of the San Francisco Psychoanalytic Institute.

Berne placed emphasis on social relationships in psychoanalysis, hence the term 'transactional' in the title. Communication is about transactions. There are three key concepts in TA (Barrow *et al.* 2001):

- anyone can change;
- everyone can think; and
- we think most effectively when we feel that we are OK and that others are OK (I'm OK, you're OK).

Other aspects of TA theory are as follows:

- strokes – positive recognition;
- life scripts – what we think about ourselves;
- drivers – what drives our thinking and feeling; and
- contracts – agreements about beneficial outcomes.

Ego states is a key concept in TA which we will examine in a little more detail in relation to classroom management. An ego state is a pattern of feeling and experience and a consistent pattern of behaviour. Berne proposed three ego states:

- the *parent* – characterised by a 'voice of authority';
- the *adult* – characterised by the ability to think and make decisions; and
- the *child* – characterised by feelings and reactions to events.

Later development of TA theory about ego states suggested that there are different types of parent and child ego states and that each type has a positive and negative element.

EXPANDED DEFINITIONS OF EGO STATES

The parent ego state:

Nurturing: the parent can nurture (+) or spoil (–)

Controlling: the parent can structure (+) or criticise (–).

The child ego state:

Adapted: the child can be co-operative (+) or resistant (–);

Free: the child can be spontaneous (+) or immature (–).

Berne suggests that we move from one ego state to another and that effective communication takes place when the response reflects the stimulus, in terms of ego states. This means that if an interaction is from a parent ego state to a child ego state, then the response should be from child ego state to parent ego state. Ego states can also be used as a means of understanding and then changing behaviour. Hellaby (2004) gives an example of the use of the concepts of ego states in a primary classroom. She describes the way in which she teaches her pupils about the ego states, using child-friendly language. For example, the controlling parent is called the 'bossy' parent, the adapted child is called the 'whingey baby' and the adult ego state is described as the thinking adult, emphasising that in this context 'adult' does not mean grown-up. Hellaby then uses a range of application activities in order to help her pupils to gain insight into their emotions and feelings, with the consequence of improved self-control. She comments:

> The behaviour in the class alters as each child becomes responsible for his/her own behaviour. If the children are not behaving appropriately. I only have to make a statement such as 'If you don't tidy up properly I will have to move into Bossy Parent' for them to shift into the appropriate ego state.

Chapter 7 of this book looks at effective communication in the classroom from an anti-oppressive practice point of view. The use of ego states and transactions from a TA perspective help us to understand how communication can either help or hinder our relationships with pupils. Being aware of and changing your own ego state should also be a consideration in helping to promote effective communication. In this perspective, classroom management is dependent on effective communication, built on self-awareness of ego states.

The theory and practice links illustrated in Table 6.3 should help you to reflect on how you and your pupils communicate.

In summary, TA applied to classroom management uses some of the key concepts discussed above in order to bring about behaviour change. The concept of ego states has been examined as an application of TA theory to classroom practice. However, the notion of behaviour change that would arise as a result of TA would be viewed differently from the behavioural perspective of behaviour change. The behavioural perspective would accept the observed behaviour change at face value, whereas the TA perspective would see it as indicative of better self-awareness ands self-regulation. In TA, the notion of 'strokes' could be equated to that of positive reinforcement, but again, there is an added 'emotional' dimension in that strokes are used to foster feelings of acceptance and belonging.

Positive discipline

Positive Discipline (Nelson *et al.* 2000) is a system of discipline that emphasises building relationships and taking responsibility. It is based on the work of Alfred Adler (1870–1937). Adler was a contemporary of Sigmund Freud but his

Table 6.3   Ego states and communication exercise

THEORY AND PRACTICE LINKS

Ego states and communication

The examples below show some typical classroom interactions. Each interaction is interpreted in the light of TA ego states and the outcome explained from this perspective.

Stimulus	Ego state	Type and whether + or –	Response	Ego state	Type and + or –	Outcome and explanation
Teacher: 'Don't do it like that, do it how I've shown you'.	Controlling parent	Critical (–)	Pupil: 'I'll do it my way'.	Adapted child	Resistant (–)	A conflict between pupil and teacher. Both have used negative ego states to communicate. One of them needs to use a different ego state to resolve the conflict: either the teacher could use controlling parent (structure) mode or the pupil should respond in adapted child mode (co-operative).
Teacher: 'OK, don't do the work if it's upsetting you'.	Nurturing parent	Spoiling (–)	Pupil: 'Great!'	Adapted child	Co-operative (+)	In this scenario the outcome for the pupil is positive and there isn't a conflict, even though there is a mismatch

in ego states. The pupil complies with the negative nurturing parent because s/he recognises that this is how to continue to have his/her needs met.

Application: over the next week, keep a diary of some exchanges between yourself and your class(es). Using the examples above as a model, fill in your own table below in order to list and analyse these exchanges from a TA ego state perspective.

Reflect on your completed table. Could the outcomes have been changed if you had adopted a different ego state? If your pupils had been aware of ego states, could they have behaved differently by using a different ego state?

Stimulus	Ego state	Type and whether + or –	Response	Ego state	Type and + or –	Outcome and explanation

Reflections on the interactions:

psychodynamic perspective is the notion of individual psychology. The term 'individual', as used by Adler, refers to the uniqueness of the individual and the importance of taking a holistic view of individuals. He was also interested in social aspects of the individual. Important concepts in Adlerian psychology, that are reflected in Positive Discipline, are as follows:

- Democracy: Adler developed training for parents that introduced the idea of the democratic parent.

- Goals: Adler stated that humans are driven by goals and that these goals are shared by society and the community;

- Choice and responsibility: the social dimension in Adler's psychology led to an emphasis on these aspects of human behaviour. In this context, behaviour is viewed in terms of its impact on others.

Positive Discipline reflects the above concepts in its construction of a democratic classroom. There are nine conditions necessary:

- order
- limits
- firmness and kindness
- student involvement
- teacher leadership
- co-operation rather than competition
- a sense of belonging
- freedom to explore and discover
- acceptable behaviour as a choice.

A *democratic teacher* uses rules and consequences, but within this framework would emphasise choice, with the aim of developing self-discipline in pupils.

Positive Discipline aims to teach responsible behaviour, via life skills or social skills programmes. Positive Discipline approaches are used to train both teachers and parents in the implementation of democratic discipline.

Psychodynamic approaches to classroom management

The two approaches described above are just a sample of the kind of approaches to classroom management that reflect a psychodynamic approach; that is, an approach which emphasises the role of feelings and emotions. In both approaches, self-awareness is the key to regulation of behaviour. Therefore, if you were to adopt a psychodynamic approach, you would place great importance on helping pupils to understand and then regulate their feelings and emotions.

This type of approach is reflected in the notion of *emotional intelligence* (EI). Perceiving and understanding emotion is a key concept in EI. It was popularised by Daniel Goleman (1995). Goleman proposed a link between emotional intelligence and success in life. Positive emotional intelligence, according to Goleman, means that pupils are socially and emotionally skilled. The role of feeling and emotion in education is now being recognised by central government:

Social, emotional and behavioural skills underlie almost every aspect of school, home and community life, including effective learning and getting on with other people. They are fundamental to school improvement. (DfES 2005)

In view of the above emphasis, a programme has been introduced for use with Foundation Stage and Key Stages 1 and 2. It is called Social and Emotional Aspects of Learning (SEAL). It shows many similarities with Goleman's ideas about emotional intelligence. For example, the five aspects of the programme are very similar to Goleman's five steps of EI, as shown below:

Goleman's five steps:

- self-awareness
- motivation
- self-regulation
- empathy
- adeptness in relationships.

SEAL's five aspects:

- self-awareness
- managing feelings
- motivation
- empathy
- social skills.

The SEAL programme is an important step in recognising the role that feeling and emotion play in learning. It is not designed as a form of troubleshooting when pupils are displaying difficulties with their emotional or behavioural development. Rather, it is intended to take a proactive, preventative approach to social and emotional development. If you have not come across this programme, we would recommend that you obtain a copy.

A humanistic and experiential perspective

Democracy in education was mentioned above in the context of Positive Discipline. The concept of democracy also forms part of the humanistic and experiential perspective of classroom management. In this perspective, the roots of the concept are found in the work of Dewey (1916). He commented: 'I believe that education . . . is a process of living and not a preparation for living'. Dewey thought that collective goals were important and that communication was an important aspect of achieving these goals. He saw education as a social process and the school as a community. Individual learning, therefore, was focused on becoming a social being who can strive for the common good.

Ideas about personal freedom and democracy were reflected in A.S. Neill's Summerhill School. The school was opened in 1921 and sought to apply the principles of humanistic education. Attendance at lessons is optional although, in practice, most pupils do choose to attend. There is a school meeting where laws are made or changed and there is no hierarchy between pupils and staff: all are treated as equals. Neill's comment about education reflects that of Dewey:

> The function of a child is to live his life – not the life his anxious parents think he should live, nor a life according to the purpose of the educator who thinks he knows what is best. (A.S Neill, cited in Lamb's 1992 edition)

The experiential psychology of Carl Rogers (Rogers and Freiberg 1994) is also an important consideration. Rogers emphasised learning via experience. Therefore, pupils should discover learning for themselves. Reflection is a key element of experiential learning. Rogers contrasted *cognitive learning*, which he called meaningless because it was not responsive to pupil needs, with *significant experiential learning*, which was responsive to learner needs.

Classroom management based on an experiential or humanistic perspective would therefore place great emphasis on meeting individual needs, but in the context of seeking the common good. Good behaviour in class would be promoted as a collective responsibility, but at the same time, imposition of disciplinary measures would not seem to fit with this approach. The focus on experience as the basis for learning might mean that pupils should experience the natural consequences of their behaviour rather than working to a set of predetermined consequences. Reflection would be important and might take the form of encouraging pupils to think about their behaviour and its consequences (especially in terms of the positive or negative impact of behaviour on the group as a whole due to the emphasis on collective responsibility).

This type of approach to classroom management might appear to be very *laissez-faire*. While it is based on some sound psychology, it is debatable whether this perspective is appropriate in the context of the demands placed on schools by central government and the culture of league tables based on pupil attainment. It could work well if pupils are very self-aware and are able to reflect on their experience. Sadly, not all pupils possess these skills, which is one of the reasons behind the development of the SEAL programme.

Making decisions about classroom managment

This chapter has looked at the way in which a range of schools of psychology would approach classroom management. One of the problems with offering such a range of perspectives is that you might feel bewildered by the choices open to you. As discussed in each section, there are advantages and disadvantages associated with all the approaches discussed, which is perhaps not helpful if you want to choose appropriate strategies for managing your class.

One way of looking at the approaches discussed is to place them on a continuum, moving from approaches that involve a high level of teacher direction and input to approaches that involve a high level of pupil decision-making. This continuum is illustrated below:

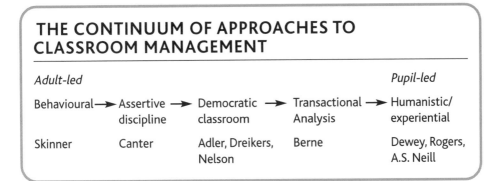

THE CONTINUUM OF APPROACHES TO CLASSROOM MANAGEMENT

Adult-led *Pupil-led*

Behavioural→ Assertive → Democratic → Transactional → Humanistic/
              discipline   classroom   Analysis   experiential

Skinner   Canter   Adler, Dreikers, Berne   Dewey, Rogers,
                           Nelson   A.S. Neill

The problem with looking at classroom management on a continuum is that it implies that teachers need to choose a point on the continuum that they feel most comfortable with. If this is the case, then it would mean that the choice would exclude all other approaches (a typical comment might be, 'If you're a behaviourist you can't have a democratic classroom').

The authors would like to suggest that classroom management should draw on a range of approaches, but have some common essential elements. The approaches described in this chapter have two such common elements: boundaries and a positive approach. Each approach tackles these elements in slightly different ways (for example, TA has 'strokes' while behavioural psychology has 'positive reinforcement'), but they are common themes. In addition to these two elements, there is no doubt that consistency is fundamental to effective classroom management. Whatever approach you implement, do it consistently.

This view of classroom management is illustrated in Figure 6.1 the 'root and branch' approach. In this model, the tree roots represent the three essential elements of classroom management: boundaries, a positive approach and consistency. Once these roots are established, the teacher can opt to move along any of the branches of the tree. We believe that this model ensures that teachers can exercise personal choice in their approach and that they will be able to implement their chosen approach effectively because they have laid solid foundations.

If you plan your classroom management using this model you will start by establishing a foundation of setting boundaries and creating a positive and consistent climate. Having done so, you can then 'experiment' with some of the strategies and approaches suggested in order to find out what is best suited to your particular situation.

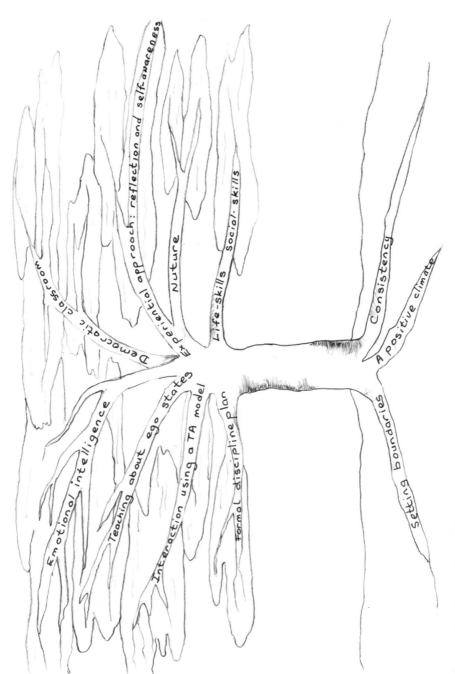

Figure 6.1 'Root and branch' model of classroom management

Summary

The purpose of this chapter was to look at strategies for managing your class. However, there will always be a small number of pupils who will need some input over and above the strategies used with the majority of pupils. We recognise, therefore, that any of the strategies and approaches you use might not be effective with all pupils. If you have pupils whose behaviour is particularly difficult or challenging, it is quite likely that you will need to take a more individualised approach. In such circumstances, you may need strategies and approaches that are beyond the remit of this book. For example, we have not covered aspects of social psychology and ecosystemic approaches in relation to the management of difficult behaviour (for further reading on these aspects of behaviour management see Miller 2003 or Tyler and Jones 1998). If you do have a particularly difficult or challenging pupil you should not hesitate to seek advice from colleagues within and outside the school.

CHAPTER 7

Communication, prejudice and equality in the classroom

Introduction and chapter aims

No doubt all professions have their hazards. For a white, male writer the educational Lorelei are surely the issues of attainment, gender, race and equal opportunities. To present a strong view one risks charges of racism, to ignore the issue, accusations of colour blindness, to present a partial view, the risk of losing one's friends. To challenge existing thinking risks all three. (adapted from Arnold 1967)

The McPherson Report (1999) defined racism in the light of the Stephen Lawrence Inquiry as follows:

racism in general terms consists of conduct or words or practices which disadvantage people because of their colour, or ethnic origin. In its more subtle form it is as damaging as in its overt form.

Most of us live and work in societies comprising people from a wide range of backgrounds. As we have discussed in a previous chapter, the ways we behave towards and communicate with each other are influenced by our perceptions. Understanding the relationship between our perception of minority groups and our behaviour towards them is vital in creating a society which promotes fairness and equality of opportunity. Prejudice linked with power can show itself as racism, sexism or homophobia and there are numerous other forms. Psychology examines human communication in a variety of ways. Some of these will be introduced in this chapter. Specifically, this chapter's aims are to examine anti-oppressive practice in relation to communication in the classroom through:

- outlining the evidence that children are not treated equally;
- describing the development of prejudice;
- examining the role of culture and development of personal identity;
- describing the phenomenon of bullying and ways of tackling it; and
- describing the insights offered from different schools of psychology.

Evidence of inequality

Evidence that pupils from different heritages have different experiences in the UK's educational system is not hard to find. Simple outcome measures such as GCSE results and exclusion rates speak for themselves. The statistics for 2002 include:

- Seventy-seven per cent of girls and 71 per cent of boys who identified themselves as Chinese achieved five or more A* to C grades.
- Thirty-eight per cent of girls and 23% of boys who identified themselves as African-Caribbean achieved five or more A* to C grades.
- Within each ethnic group a higher proportion of girls than boys achieved five or more A* to C grades at GCSE.
- The permanent exclusion rate of 42 per 10,000 for pupils who identified themselves as Black Caribbean was three times that for White pupils.
- Pupils who identified themselves as Chinese and Indian had the lowest exclusion rates at two per 10,000 and three per 10,000 respectively.

(Source: National Statistics online)

The list could be longer.

In spite of the growth of new technologies, education in schools is still dominated by communications between adults and children. Psychology has illuminated the nature of human communication from a number of different perspectives. We begin with a simple study based in behavioural psychology.

Insights from behavioural psychology

Recall that the raw material of behavioural psychology consists of *observation*. We consider what people *do* rather than what they *say* they do. A second principle is the recognition of the roles that antecedents and consequences of behaviour play in determining that behaviour. If behaviour is followed by a reward it is more likely to be repeated; if it is followed by a negative re-enforcement, it is less likely to be repeated. An application of this school can be found in classroom observation of the communications teachers have with children. Hathiwala-Ward and Swinson (1999) examined the ways teachers communicate with pupils from different cultures in a small but systematic study.

Teachers were observed in their interactions with children. Four particular communications were counted:

- positive comments about children's work;
- negative comments about children's work;
- positive comments about children's behaviour; and
- negative comments about children's behaviour.

These categories have been used in studies over more than twenty years. A more comprehensive account is described in Chapter 6.

The school population declared themselves as 4 per cent Asian UK, 17 per cent Black UK and 75 per cent White, and eight classes were observed with 243 pupils in total. The results are disturbing:

- Teachers directed significantly more verbal attention to Black UK pupils.
- Teachers' use of positive feedback was the same for all groups.
- Teachers used significantly more negative feedback for Black UK pupils.
- Teachers' use of positive feedback for work was the same for all pupils.
- Teachers' use of positive feedback for behaviour was the same for all pupils.
- Teachers' use of negative feedback for work was the same for all pupils.
- Teachers used significantly more negative feedback for behaviour for Black UK pupils.

The authors speculated that the results in their study arose from two factors. First, the tendency for teachers to view Black pupils as potential troublemakers, and secondly, the use of negative strategies in dealing with the pupils perceived as potentially difficult. The authors suggest that there may be some justification for alienated Black young people feeling 'picked on'.

The study was small-scale, and in a school with a small proportion of pupils from minority cultures, but it does point to the probability of some pupils having a very different (and negative) experience of education as a result of different patterns of communication between teachers and pupils.

The authors cite additional studies in monocultural schools in which teachers were invited to nominate their 'ten worst behaved students'. When observed, not only did the students receive a disproportionate amount of negative feedback, but they also received almost no *positive* feedback at all.

Behavioural psychology emphasises the *antecedents* and *consequences* of behaviour. Antecedents include rules. Rules can be culturally biased; insisting on the removal of head clothes in school can be offensive to some cultures. Similarly, rewards may not be viewed in the same way. A school offering McDonald's vouchers to teenagers who may only eat Halal meat (or be very concerned about their weight) may inadvertently be biased away from some groups of children. One secondary school known to the authors introduced a reward system with a bicycle as the greatest reward. The school had a small (but significant) population of children in wheelchairs. The school inadvertently failed to include this group in the reward system. A reward is only successful if it is perceived as rewarding by the recipient.

Praise and correction ratios in class

Try to count the number of positive and negative statements you make to different pupils. What are the ratios of positive to negative comments? Look at the allocation of rewards. Are these different for different groups?

Insights from cognitive psychology

Behind the different patterns of communication between teachers and pupils lie different mental processes. Cognitive psychology offers insights into the mental processes underpinning categorisation, attitudes and prejudice. There are two essential elements:

- separation of self from others; and
- establishment of stereotypes.

Separation of self from others

There have been significant studies of this element. In particular, the Sherif and Sherif summer camp studies have been seminal in advancing our understanding of separation and group identity. Sherif and Sherif (1956) used the traditional US summer camps for children as the setting for their studies. They contrived three different conditions:

Condition 1: Children were divided into different groups. Children who had shown friendship towards each other were separated. The groups were given names and joint tasks to perform. As expected, the friendships tended to be within these groups rather than based on historic patterns.

Condition 2: The groups were established as in condition 1. However, an element of competition was introduced. Teams competed for points and there were winners and losers. The competitions were arranged so that the teams were always close together. The teams began to show hostility. If you were in the same team, you were 'in'; if you were in the other team you were 'out'.

Condition 3: The groups were given joint tasks to perform. A third group was introduced. The teams started to co-operate and exclude the new group. The teams converged to exclude the 'common enemy'.

The study is often cited to describe the development of 'in group' and 'out group' members.

Groups in classes

Consider the ways that children are grouped in classes. Are there ways in which 'in groups' and 'out groups' can be encouraged/discouraged? What are the advantages and disadvantages of this?

Establishment of stereotypes

The establishment of stereotypes has also been well reported. The 'halo' effect discussed in Chapter 5 can be extended to include perception of different items. Perhaps the clearest example of this is provided by Tajfel and Wilkes (1963). They presented subjects with two sets of four lines, but presented in different ways:

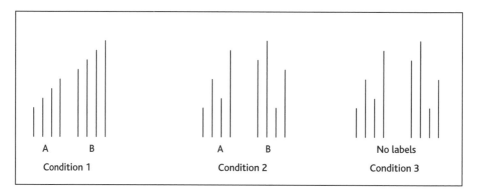

Figure 7.1 Stimulus materials used by Tajfel and Wilkes (1963)

Subjects were asked to judge the lengths of the lines in each of the pairs. In condition 1, subjects exaggerated the differences. They formed *stereotypes* for the two groups. Group A has shorter lines than group B. In condition 2, the subjects again exaggerated the differences, but in condition 3 they did not. The only difference between conditions 2 and 3 was the presence of the label; so we can conclude that the label, not the lines, contributed to the stereotyping of the two groups. The researchers concluded that stereotypes require both *differences* and *labels*. Both of these conditions are met when considering children from different heritages and can lead to the different styles of communication described above. Only by understanding these processes can we begin to create educational environments which promote fairness in communication.

Studies of the development of racial stereotypes and prejudice in children exist. Augustinos and Rosewarne (2001) presented a compelling example. Working in Australia, they examined the development of the distinction between racial stereotype and prejudicial beliefs in children between 5/6 years and 8/9 years. They surveyed studies to show that white children as young as 3 and 4 are able to demonstrate racial and ethnic awareness. A consistent finding is the preference for white as opposed to black skin among majority groups. White skin is assigned favourable or positive characteristics, while black is negative. These attributions decline with age. In their study they tested five predictions of the differences between stereotype knowledge and prejudice:

1   Children will demonstrate knowledge of cultural stereotypes and attribute positive adjectives to white stimuli and negative adjectives to black stimuli.

2   Children aged 5/6 will show little difference between knowledge of cultural stereotypes and personal knowledge.

3   Children aged 8/9 will demonstrate differences between their stereotype knowledge and personal beliefs. When assessing black stimuli they are more likely to endorse negative adjectives as stereotypes than as personal beliefs.

4   Prejudice will decline with age: 8/9-year-olds are less likely to endorse negative evaluations of black stimuli than 5/6-year-olds.

5   Both age groups will demonstrate 'racial awareness' by discriminating between white and black stimuli and identifying which one looks most like them.

The distinction between cultural stereotype and personal belief was made by asking what *other* people thought or believed as opposed to what *they* thought or believed. The study found evidence for all five hypotheses. Only the fourth failed to demonstrate the differences usually considered adequate for statistical purposes, but the differences were in the directions predicted. As far as the authors are aware, this study has not been replicated in educational areas catering for children from different heritages.

In an American study, Littleford *et al.* (2005) examined anxiety in white pupils when partnered with students from different heritages. The measures included self-report and cardio-vascular responses. As expected, white students were less comfortable and more anxious when paired with those from other heritages compared with same-heritage pairing.

In an Australian study, Nguy and Hunt (2004) examined bullying and ethnicity. They cited previous studies which reported rates of up to 76 per cent of ethnic minority students being bullied because of their ethnicity, although other studies drew a distinction between perceptions of bullying rather than actual reports of bullying frequency. Their study was conducted in a school in Sydney in which the ethnic majority was 37 per cent of the school population. This majority would identify themselves as 'anglo'. The minority groups were from the Middle East (19%), east Asian (13%) and mixed or other (13%). This study did not find differences in bullying in different ethnic groups; it did find *small* differences in attitudes towards bullying. Ethnic minority groups were slightly less favourable towards bullying than the majority. The authors conclude that the multicultural policies of the school were having some success.

Behaviour and culture

Consider a pupil who is causing some trouble in class at the moment. Are there differences in background between them and a) other pupils; b) members of staff?

To what extent does knowledge about these differences help understand the behaviour of the child?

Experimental evidence of bias

The following studies point to differential communication resulting from the development of racial bias. American studies of racial bias have tended to focus on adults. Dovidio and Gaertner (1986) looked at the treatment of African Americans by European Americans who denounced racial prejudice. In spite of the rhetoric, there were differences in treatment. The authors concluded that these must arise from subconscious processes. The work has similarities to a landmark study from the 1930s, by LaPiere. At that time there were no anti-discrimination laws in the US, and white-only bars, restaurants and hotels were commonplace. He surveyed 120 hotels and 92 per cent indicated that they would not accept Chinese guests. However, when a Chinese couple who spoke good English and were very skilled socially approached the establishment they were accepted in all except one of the hotels. The study is cited as evidence that people may say one thing, yet behave in a different way.

Implicit biases in majority and minority groups of children have been explored through the use of ambiguous figures. Children are shown images of children which can be interpreted in different ways. European-American children judged the actions of African-American children more negatively than the actions of European-American children. The African-American children either showed no bias (Lawrence 1991) or negative bias towards the African-American children (Sagar and Schofield 1980). More recently, however, McGlothlin *et al.* (2005) found that children attending racially and ethnically heterogeneous schools did not demonstrate racial bias when interpreting children's intentions towards commit-ting moral transgressions towards other children. However, bias was found when children were asked about potential friendship. European-American children were less likely to suggest that the characters could be friends when the potential transgressor was Black. This effect seemed to increase with age, with ten-year-olds showing more bias than six-year-olds. Killen *et al.* (2005) investigated attitudes in minority groups using the ambiguous figure method. They found no differences in evaluations of cross-race friendship potential; however, white children were more likely to be viewed as transgressors than Black children in certain situations.

Children were asked to rate the similarities between children. The results suggest that children evaluated shared interests in sport as indicative of similarity rather than race or colour. These findings were repeated when exploring reasons for potential friendship. Very few children used race or skin colour as a reason why children could or could not be friends, although children who did use ethnicity as a reason for judging peers to be similar were less likely to judge that the cross-race children could be friends.

These studies were conducted in the USA. The extent to which their findings might be replicated in the UK is questionable, but we have to conclude that the phenomenon of racial bias in children is complex but does exist.

Identity

We discussed earlier the distinction between 'I' and 'me'. The development of an identity must now be explored. For children in school, the social interactions and communications will be influenced by a sense of identity.

> **REFLECTION POINT**
>
> **Self and culture**
>
> Write down a description of yourself. Try to include as many elements as you can. Then cross out those that are defined by your cultural or ethnic origins. What is left?

Culture is central to our perception of ourselves and the defining of selfhood. I cannot meaningfully separate me from my culture. It underpins communication.

From birth, two complementary processes occur. *Socialisation* describes the tendency to establish and maintain relationships with others while *individuation* describes the development of our sense of self and the creation of a space for ourselves in the existing social order. Children are born with processes designed to engage with care-givers. They seek out areas of high visual contrast, like eyes. They turn their heads to suckle objects touching their faces and are able to express feelings of comfort and discomfort. A young baby's cry is interpreted as a request for help.

The foundations of social identity are laid from birth. Shaffer (1984) has proposed a developmental scheme which serves to remind us just how basic the processes are within the first two years of life.

1   During the immediate post-birth period the priorities for carers are to regularise the infant's basic biological processes such as sleep and feeding so that they become harmonised with the environmental requirements.

2   From about two months, the infant shows an increase in attentiveness to the external world, in particular to people. Face-to-face interactions between infant and adult become central features for both adult and infant.

3 From about five months, the infant's manipulative skills develop and attention shifts from people to objects.

4 From about eight months the infant's behaviour becomes more flexible with reciprocity and intentionality becoming apparent. The relationship with the care-giver becomes more symmetrical.

5 From the middle of the second year the capacity for symbolic representation gradually emerges. Words are used in social interactions and the child's self-awareness grows.

Within this framework we see the importance of the child's prime care-givers in shaping the experiences and potential sense of selfhood and identity.

Two other processes serve to promote and maintain our membership of a cultural group: conformity and obedience.

Conformity

The social psychologist Solomon Asch devised a simple experiment in the 1950s in which a subject was asked to state which of three lines was the same length as a fourth. The discrimination was simple. The subject was sat in a room with eight others, all of whom gave the same, but incorrect, answer. The subject was the last to speak. Thirty-two per cent of the subjects changed what they were going to say to conform to the majority. Those who did not reported unease and disturbance. A subsequent experiment by Berenda (in Sherif and Sherif 1956) with children aged between 7 and 10 found that the influence of the majority was significantly greater. Perhaps surprisingly, though, the children were less distressed by the experiment than were the adults. Asch's work is cited as evidence for the need of humans to be part of a group.

An example of this in a classroom can be found in a sex education lesson in which a pupil claims that you can't get pregnant the first time you have unprotected sex with somebody. Other pupils will agree, and a belief emerges that this is true.

Obedience

Stanley Milgram investigated the degree to which an adult might be persuaded to harm another at the request of a third party. He created a fake laboratory in which subjects were told that they were studying 'memory'. On arriving at the lab, the subject found a second 'subject' (actually a confederate of Milgram). The second 'subject' was strapped into a machine that purported to deliver electric shocks. There was a meter visible, which suggested the voltage being delivered. It went from 15 to 450 volts. The second 'subject' made mistakes and the experimenter required the subject to press a button that apparently delivered an electric shock. As the meter rose, the second 'subject' began to scream. The shocks were fake, but this was not known to the subject. Sixty-five per cent of the subjects continued to deliver 'shocks' up to the maximum of 450 volts. Milgram suggested that the predilication for obedience to authority was probably a necessary requirement for communal life and built into our species by evolution. The influence of powerful people close to the individual, needs to be understood.

If we apply this to education we can see these effects present in a number of settings. Teachers attend review meetings for children with special needs. Present at the meeting are usually the teacher, the special needs co-ordinator, the parent, a representative from the local educational authority (often an educational psychologist) and, sometimes, the child. If there are difficulties to be raised, those at the meeting may start to make suggestions. Usually, the last person to comment is the parent. If all the professionals agree, the pressure on the parent to conform (and obey) is very great. (For a more comprehensive analysis of this phenomenon, see Arnold and Yeomans 2005, p.162 ff.)

Both conformity and obedience are cited as processes that assist humans to be members of groups and, therefore, the ways in which people communicate. Identity is associated with membership of a group. It seems likely that this has biological origins.

Insights from biological perspectives

Recall that this school of psychology emphasises the biological commonality across cultures. So insights from this school tend to play down cultural differences, except when they impact on the chances of survival of the individual or the reproduction of genes. Post-puberty behaviours may be influenced by these factors. These can be described as:

- defence; and
- display.

If an individual feels threatened, they will respond. If somebody similar to that individual is perceived to be threatened, the degree of response will be proportionate to the similarity. Biologically, young people may behave in ways which maximise their opportunities to promote their genetic material. This may result in gender differences. Behaviours suggesting jealousy, rivalry, hatred and aggression may have biological bases. The children displaying these may not be aware of their function. Classroom applications of these ideas include removing an angry child from the audience provided by the rest of a class and using group work to help pupils to become aware of the processes involved.

Insights from psychodynamic psychology

Communication in class can be influenced by sources of which the people concerned are unaware. Teachers talk about children 'pressing our buttons'. Some children seem to 'get to us'. There is 'something about that child' that annoys us. Psychodynamic theory suggests that these apparently irrational thoughts arise from fear. This fear may be about an aspect of ourselves or someone else. When working with teachers and parents for whom a child has 'got to them', psychologists often find the following comments:

'S/he's just like me at that age and I wish that I had done better.'

'S/he's like my cousin who ended up in a mental institution.'

'I was good at school. These children *ought* to behave the way I did. It's not fair. *I* didn't get rewarded for behaviour, so why should they?'

There is some empirical support for the assumption that people have *unconscious* thoughts and ideas. These may influence and impede our communications with people who may be different. Recall that one of the assumptions made by this school is the existence of internal psychological processes to defend us from anxiety. These *defence mechanisms* distort our internal visions of the world and keep certain conflicts away from our conscious selves. By so doing, they can create apparently irrational beliefs and behaviours. Groups of people who are not like us can create anxiety and, therefore, our perceptions, communications and behaviours may appear irrational.

THEORY AND PRACTICE LINKS

An examination of children who 'get to you'

Can you think of a child who has 'got to you'? List the ways in which this child is both like and different from you. Does this illuminate why this child has 'got to you'?

We will use the issue of homophobia to illustrate these points. However, the same processes apply to children or adults from other groups.

Robertson and Monsen (2001) remind us that records of homosexual behaviour are found in all areas of culture and history. Classical Greek society celebrated it in art and literature as did other civilisations such as Chinese, Indian and Middle Eastern. Although harsh penalties for homosexual behaviour were instituted after the Black Death, these came from fears that such behaviour would be a threat to repopulating Europe. The cultural taboos in the Old Testament only became widespread after the Greek Bible was translated into English in the seventeenth century when the behaviour was widely seen as deviant and immoral. It was classified as a disease by the International Classification of Diseases until 1992. It was found in the Diagnostic and Statistical Manual of Mental Illnesses until 1973. There is still a view held by some that it is curable.

Psychodynamic psychology offers a number of insights. The cultural transmission of the taboo can translate into irrational thoughts such as 'It's dirty' or 'It's the same as child sexual abuse'. Homophobia is defined as: 'the dread of being in close quarters with homosexuals – and in the case of homosexuals themselves, self-loathing' (Weinberg 1973, in Crowley *et al.* 2001).

There is a debate whether it is better described as a phobia or 'anti-homosexual prejudice'. An insight offered by psychodynamic psychology includes the defences against identification. People defend themselves against the thought or feeling that they might, too, be attracted to a same-sex partner. There is some empirical support for this view. Lohr *et al.* (1997) reported higher rates of sexual arousal to homoerotic images in men who professed homophobic views than those who did not.

It is possible to become aware of these mental processes, but until such self-awareness is achieved, the individual is likely to continue to think and behave in irrational ways. This is particularly relevant in adolescence. Rivers (2001) surveyed the types of bullying experienced at school by gay, bisexual and transgendered men, and lesbian and bisexual women. Eighty-five per cent of the men reported being called names (69% of women) with 75 per cent of men reporting being ridiculed in front of others (54% women).

Bullying

All schools are required by law to have an anti-bullying policy that complies with the Human Rights Act 1998 and the Race Relations (Amendment) Act 2000. However bullying is an aspect of behaviour that occurs in all schools. It is a form of communication between the people concerned. The extent to which it occurs in school will depend on the quality, consistency and effectiveness of the school's anti-bullying policy.

The implication of the above is that teachers are likely to come into contact with bullies and their victims. Although it is a whole-school responsibility for preventing and dealing with bullying, it is nevertheless important that individual teachers have an awareness of bullying. It is possible that you will be the first point of contact for a parent or pupil who has a complaint about bullying. In addition, being aware of the signs of bullying might help you to intervene.

What is bullying?

The definition offered by Olweus (1993) is one most commonly cited by researchers. Olweus defines bullying as showing three characteristics:

- it involves some form of aggressive behaviour;
- it takes place over time and is repeated; and
- it involves an imbalance of power.

The notion that bullying involves aggression does not mean that this type of behaviour is always overtly physical. Aggression is seen here in very broad terms. Bullying behaviour is often categorised into physical, verbal and indirect, all of which are forms of aggression. *Physical bullying* involves behaviour such as hitting, kicking, pinching, and so on. *Verbal bullying* involves behaviour such as teasing or name-calling. *Indirect bullying* involves actions such as name-calling or sending offensive mobile phone text messages.

Bullying can take a number of forms. Often an individual who is bullied is different (or is perceived to be different) in some way from his or her peers. However, it is important that within this wide remit a number of specific forms of bullying are identified. Examples are racist bullying, sexual bullying, homophobic bullying (different from sexual bullying in that the focus is on the sexual orientation (or perceived orientation) of the individual) and bullying based on perceptions of special educational needs or disabilities.

Rigby (2004) suggests five theoretical perspectives in the definition of bullying. These are useful to consider as the perspective taken will lead to different ways of tackling the problem. Rigby's five perspectives and related types of intervention are as follows:

- The *individual differences* perspective. This focuses on notions of oppression of a weaker individual by a stronger individual and therefore emphasises the characteristics of bullies and victims. Bullies are thought to be physically strong, aggressive and lacking in empathy. Victims are thought to be physically weak, to have low self-esteem and to be quiet and withdrawn. Intervention focuses on modifying the behaviours of both bullies and victims.

- The *developmental perspective*. This views bullying as a developmental process, part of 'growing up' and the process of the child learning how to assert him/herself. It also recognises that forms of bullying change developmentally, with direct physical aggression more common in younger children. There is a danger in adopting this perspective as it might lead schools into deciding not to tackle bullying. Glover *et al.* point out that this is a potential problem: 'Many staff still appear to believe that all except the most serious bullying is part of the process of growing up, and action on all fronts to reduce reported anti-social behaviour merely serves to heighten awareness of "something which has always been there" '. Although this perspective might initially suggest that it encourages a lack of action, a developmental perspective would help schools to take action in relation to types of bullying that are more prevalent at different ages. Therefore, KS1 and KS2 might emphasise direct bullying, whilst KS3 and KS4 might emphasise indirect bullying. In order to refute the notion that bullying can be explained away as a stage of development, Elinoff *et al.* (2004) suggest that bullying is seen as part of a continuum of behaviour that includes low-level behaviours which might otherwise be considered as developmental and therefore not as being bullying.

- *The socio-cultural perspective.* This emphasises the relative power of different social groups, based on factors such as race, social status or gender. Interventions based on this perspective will emphasise teaching related to prejudice and discrimination, in order to increase toleration of individual differences.

- *The peer pressure perspective.* This also has a social context, but relates specifically to the school community. The behaviours and attitudes of that school community will influence individuals and therefore make bullying more or less likely to take place. Intervention based on this perspective would emphasise work with groups of pupils who are potential or actual bullies in order to reduce any peer pressure that might reinforce bullying behaviour.

- The *restorative justice perspective.* This perspective looks at bullying from the standpoint of shame and remorse. An individual who bullies is viewed as lacking these qualities and, as a consequence, does not feel part of a community. Therefore, intervention emphasises notions such as responsibility, citizenship and the development of positive peer relationships.

THEORY AND PRACTICE LINKS

An examination of your anti-bullying policy

All schools must have an anti-bullying policy.

Find the policy for your school.

Look at it in the context of the five perspectives outlined above.

Does the policy reflect any specific perspective?

Do you think that other perspectives should be reflected in the policy and, if so, which ones?

Signs of bullying

As a class teacher, form tutor or subject teacher you have day-to-day contact with your pupils. Therefore, you might spot changes in behaviour or demeanour that are indicative of bullying. In addition, parents might report some of these signs to you as they are more likely to be apparent in a home context. The list below is not exhaustive but does give many of the signs that might indicate that a pupil is a victim of bullying. Often, these will be changes from the pupil's usual behaviour:

- changes is attendance pattern: non-attendance, non-attendance on certain days, truanting from particular lessons, not wanting to attend school;

- appearing generally unhappy, withdrawn or anxious;
- health problems: headaches, sickness (vomiting), sleeplessness;
- being frightened of travelling to school;
- losing possessions and money; asking for money from parents (or taking money from them); and
- poor or reduced appetite.

Dealing with and preventing bullying

If you detect any of the above signs and they are a change from the 'norm' in terms of the pupil's usual behaviour and demeanour it is important that you take action. If you are not confident about speaking with the pupil directly, take advice from staff in school: for example, staff with pastoral responsibility, a member of the senior management team, head of year or your mentor (if you have one). If you do speak with the pupil, avoid putting ideas into his or her head (for example, by asking 'Are you being bullied?' or 'Who is bullying you?'). The way in which you elicit information will depend on the age of the child. The DfES anti-bullying package 'Don't Suffer in Silence' (DfES 2002) gives five key points that are helpful:

- never ignore suspected bullying;
- don't make premature assumptions;
- listen carefully to what all pupils have to say (just because all accounts agree does not mean that they are truthful);
- adopt a problem-solving approach that moves pupils on from justifying themselves; and
- follow up repeatedly in order to make sure that any bullying is not continuing.

Preventing bullying is also important. Prevention should not be the sole responsibility of individual teachers. However, there are steps that you can take to try to make sure that bullying does not happen in your class. The website www.antibullying.net suggests that subtle and indirect bullying can be a common feature of a classroom and is difficult for the teacher to detect (for example, the way in which one pupil looks at another can be intimidating). In order to prevent this kind of classroom climate, the website suggests a 'non-violent classroom'. In this type of classroom, bullying is discussed openly and pupils are left in no doubt that the teacher will deal with any incidents. The teacher also models appropriate behaviour and interactions via use of a fair and consistent discipline system. Tackling 'bystander behaviour' as part of class discussions about bullying can help. Camodeca and Goossens (2005) suggest that the intervention of a bystander can be an effective strategy in dealing with bullying.

Attention to friendships in class might be another useful strategy. Bollmer *et al.* (2005) suggest that quality of friendships plays a role in preventing bullying. Having a good-quality 'best friend' protects potential victims from bullying. Furthermore, such quality relationships can prevent individuals from becoming perpetrators, since the friendship gives a model of a positive peer relationship and helps in the learning of social skills.

It must be emphasised that preventing and dealing with bullying is a whole-school responsibility. If you are presented with a complaint of bullying from a parent or pupil, it is your individual responsibility, in the first instance, to follow up the complaint. However, you should always make sure that other members of staff are informed so that appropriate action is taken and the incident is logged (most local education authorities require schools to log incidents). There is a range of methods for preventing and dealing with bullying, but it is outside the scope of this section to examine these in detail. We would urge you to obtain a copy of the DfES package that was sent to all maintained schools. It is also available on line (access the DfES website – www.dfes.gov.uk – and follow the links). Make sure you have a copy of the school's anti-bullying policy and find out the referral route you need to follow in order to report incidents.

THEORY AND PRACTICE LINKS

Tackling bullying

We would suggest you undertake this activity after reading the DfES package and consulting your school policy.

In your lesson planning, identify a suitable session for a class activity or discussion about bullying. It might be a specific PSE/PSHE lesson, a form period or a circle time 'slot'.

Plan a lesson that focuses on bullying. Decide on the message that you want to convey and how you will do it. There are a number of different foci that you can choose, for example:

● what bullying as;
● what to do if you see someone being bullied;
● how to be assertive; and
● the importance of telling someone you are being bullied.

If you are working with young children you might consider the use of puppets or stories as the basis for your lesson. With older pupils, age-appropriate stories can be useful or a straight discussion format, possibly using fictitious scenarios as a prompt for discussion.

Evaluate your lesson and use your reflections to plan further opportunities for raising the issue of bullying.

Summary

Communication in schools is underpinned by hidden psychological processes and is set in a cultural context. Different psychological schools suggest different elements for combatting prejudice and promoting positive communication between teachers, pupils and parents:

Behavioural psychology

- Count the frequency and balance of praise/rewards and corrections for each of the different groups.
- Consider the nature of the rewards. A reward is only rewarding if it is valued by the recipient.
- Look at the antecedents for different groups. Are the rules biased in favour of one group rather than another?

Cognitive psychology

- Look out for bias in perceptions of behaviour and the assumptions behind them. We tend to feel more comfortable with people like us.
- Be aware of the difference in knowledge that we have of different groups. Assumptions that pupils will understand in the same way cannot be sustained.
- Sensitively employ positive role models from the different cultures.

Experiential psychology

- Elicit children's experiences of school in an open-ended way.
- Provide opportunities for different groups to relate areas of their own culture to others.
- Elicit concepts of fairness from children. Social justice is usually a high priority for children.
- Involve children in the running of the school through school councils, peer mediation and mentoring.

Biological psychology

- Accept that there will be gender differences.
- Recognise the universal nature of wanting to reproduce.
- Behaviour in school may have an element of display, to attract a potential partner.

Psychodynamic psychology

- Examine your own beliefs about minority groups.
- Be aware that there may be unconscious processes which distort your perception of the groups.
- If children 'get to you', look for unusual similarities in yourself and others.

CHAPTER 8

Monitoring and assessment

Introduction and chapter aims

During the course of your teaching career you will be expected to monitor and assess pupil progress on a very regular basis. Monitoring and assessment is covered by many standards within QTS, which gives an indication of the importance of these activities in the professional duties of the teacher.

The aims of this chapter are as follows:

- to examine what is meant by monitoring and assessment, by looking at some of the psychological theories underpinning these terms; and
- to look at the purposes, types and methods of assessment from a psychological perspective.

What is assessment?

This might seem to be a strange starting point. Assessment is a very common term used by a wide range of individuals involved in education (parents, teachers, classroom assistants, pupils, to name a few), so surely we know what we mean? The problem is that the word is one that is used so frequently that we rarely stop to think about what we mean when we use it. It is one of those terms that we assume has a shared meaning for all users.

This chapter is not going to assume that we know what is meant by assessment; therefore, we will begin by establishing a meaning for the word.

The derivation of the word 'assessment' is the Latin *assidere*, which means to sit beside. Although this is the derivation of the word, dictionary definitions tend to focus on notions of evaluation, or determining value. The range of definitions and meanings for assessment are related to the purpose that it fulfils. Therefore, the following suggestions below for what is meant by assessment will apply in specific contexts.

- obtaining evidence;
- measurement;
- classification;
- placement;
- determining effectiveness;
- determining performance;
- determining what to teach next.

The QCA website distinguishes between short-, medium- and long-term assessment. Short-term assessment takes place on a day-to-day basis; medium-term assessment looks at progress against key learning objectives and would take place approximately every half-term. Long-term assessment takes place at the end of every academic year and would also involve statutory assessments in years 2, 6 and 9.

Distinguishing between assessment *of* learning and assessment *for* learning

Scrutiny of the Department for Education and Skills (DfES) and Qualification and Curriculum Authority (QCA) websites did not find a definition of assessment. However, there is a distinction made between assessment *for* learning and assessment *of* learning. Assessment *for* learning (AFL) is a major initiative for both primary and secondary education that emphasises the use of assessment to improve learning. It is defined as:

> The process of seeking and interpreting evidence for use by learners and their teachers to decide where the learners are in their learning, where they need to go and how best to get there. (DfES 2004).

The Assessment Reform Group (1999) identifies several characteristics of AFL, which are as follows:

- it is embedded in teaching and learning;
- it involves sharing learning goals with pupils and telling pupils the standards they are aiming for;
- it involves self-assessment;
- it involves feedback;
- it promotes confidence; and
- it involves the teacher and pupils in reviewing and reflecting on assessment data.

Four major themes in AFL are identified (Black *et al.* 2002), as follows:

- questioning: framing questions that are worth asking, allowing time for pupils to respond, extending understanding and careful thought about the purpose of asking questions;

- feedback through marking: encouraging pupil development, giving guidance, allowing pupils opportunities to follow up comments and giving feedback to provoke thought;

- peer and self-assessment: transparent evaluation criteria, teaching peer assessment, pupils assessing own progress and recognition of the unique contribution that peer and self-assessment can make; and

- the formative use of summative tests: encouraging pupil reflection to help plan revision; allowing pupils to set questions and mark answers; promoting pupil's understanding of how work can be improved; and seeing summative tests as a positive part of the learning process.

Assessment purposes

The list of meanings of assessment given above show that assessment can be defined according to its purpose. That is why there are a number of ways of defining the term. This is also reflected by the distinction made between assessment of and for learning.

The variety of assessment purposes can be summarised into five main categories: formative, summative, diagnostic, ipsative and evaluative. Each purpose will be examined in this section.

Formative assessment

Formative assessment provides ongoing feedback about pupil progress, in order to ensure that further learning and development take place. It is a process that helps pupils to learn. Formative assessment would equate to the short-term assessment described above. The key questions that formative assessment asks are:

- What do pupils know already?
- What do pupils need to do next?

Some similarities between formative assessment and AFL are apparent, in that both types of assessment are designed to have an impact on learning. Marking is an example of formative assessment; see, for example, Jerram et al.'s (1988) work about responsive and corrective feedback to children's written work.

Pause, Prompt and Praise (PPP: McNaughton, Glynn and Robinson 1987) is an example of formative assessment in the context of hearing pupils read. It is a tutoring procedure designed to give feedback on errors as pupils read text. The procedure is illustrated in Figure 8.1.

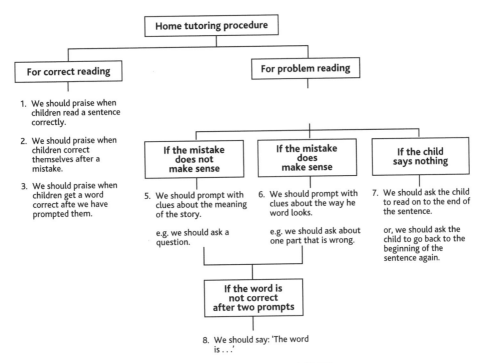

Figure 8.1   Pause, prompt, praise (from McNaughton *et al.* 1987)

Studies over a number of years have shown that PPP is a very effective means of accelerating progress in reading. It has been used successfully by parents, teachers, classroom assistants and peer tutors.

Find out more about Pause Prompt and Praise

See the reference list for details of the original *Pause, Prompt, Praise* (McNaughton *et al.* 1987), plus:

Allington, R. (2005) *What Really Matters for Struggling Readers.* Harlow: Pearson.

Wearmouth, J., Soler, J. and Reid, G. (eds) (2002) *Addressing Difficulties in Literacy Development: Responses at Family, Pupil and Teacher Level.* London: Routledge.

The Literacy Trust website contains some useful information: www.literacytrust.org.uk

---

Summative assessment

Summative assessment is carried out after a period of teaching has taken place, in order to find out what or how much has been learned. Summative assessment would equate to medium- or long-term assessment described above. The key questions that summative assessment asks are:

● What have pupils learned?

● How much have they learned?

● How well have pupils performed in comparison with set standards?

Tests and examinations are examples of summative assessment. Generally, summative assessments do not help to inform the next steps of teaching as they are carried out at the end of a unit of work. For example, a GCSE examination is a summative assessment that takes place at the end of a two-year period of work related to a set syllabus.

Diagnostic assessment

Diagnostic assessment is carried out in order to find out what a pupil already knows or can do. The information is then used to plan teaching and learning opportunities that meet the pupil's needs. The key questions that diagnostic assessment asks are:

- In relation to a specific skill, set of skills or curriculum area, what can the pupil do and what can't the pupil do?

- What do I therefore need to teach?

A simple diagnostic assessment would be to ask a pupil to read a list of 50 high-frequency sight words. This would result in a number for words read correctly and incorrectly which then identifies which words should be taught in the pupil's word recognition programme.

Miscue analysis is an example of a diagnostic assessment. It is a way of noting and analysing a pupil's reading in order to pinpoint strengths and weaknesses.

Find out more about miscue analysis

An information leaflet about miscue analysis can be obtained from: The United Kingdom Literacy Association (www.ukla.org), or Upton House, Baldock Street, Royston, Herts, SG8 5AY.

Ipsative assessment

Ipsative assessment is where a pupil's performance is measured against his or her prior performance. It can be equated with the notion of 'personal best'. The key questions that ipsative assessment asks are:

- How did I do today?

- How did today's performance compare with yesterday's?

An example of ipsative assessment might be where all class members are given a spelling test with the aim that pupils increase their own score from one week to the next.

Evaluative assessment

Evaluative assessment is used to find out about the effectiveness of a particular approach, strategy or type of teaching. The key questions that evaluative assessment ask are:

- Did this innovation work?

- How well did it work?

- Do the results indicate that I should carry on with this innovation or should I abandon it?

- What difference did this innovation make?

Examples of evaluative assessment are more likely to be found at a whole-school level than in relation to individual classrooms. An example of an evaluative assessment might be where a school introduces a new reading programme for failing readers. Pupils would be assessed before and after the programme was introduced in order to find out what impact the programme has on their reading progress.

What is assessment?: summary and application exercise

A definition of assessment is related to the assessment purpose, although it almost always involves some kind of judgement. In terms of implications for teaching, you will need to be clear about *why* you are assessing your pupils. Sometimes the purpose will be out of your control, such as when SATs are administered or where your school administers a reading test in order to monitor standards year-on-year. However, when assessment decisions are under your control, clarity is important. A useful maxim to bear in mind is that *assessment should make a difference to your pupils*. The application exercise below should help you to match assessment purposes to a range of questions about teaching and learning in your classroom.

THEORY AND PRACTICE LINKS

Assessment purposes application activity

Below are a number of statements or questions that arise from a range of teaching situations. Match each statement or question to one of the five assessment purposes covered (formative, summative, diagnostic, ipsative, evaluative).

Thomas is a new pupil in my teaching group or class. I need to find out what he does and doesn't know about my subject.

What have my class learned about the Tudors?

Sally is finding multiplication difficult to grasp. I need to find out more about her number skills.

Has teaching spelling in word families worked?

Should Arfan start work on learning set two high-frequency words?

Is Kieran's reading better than it was at the start of the year?

Has Emma beaten her score in today's test of chemical formulae?

I've marked Arun's human geography essay and written some pointers to help him with the next assignment.

Types of assessment 1: norm-referenced assessment

Norm-referenced assessment compares a pupil's performance with his or her peers and comprises a comprehensive technology for making comparisons and determining individual differences. This type of assessment arises from the cognitive school of psychology, which is interested in mental processes. Norm-referenced assessment is one way in which psychologists can measure and classify these mental processes.

The particular assessment methods associated with norm-referenced assessment are called *standardised tests*. A standardised test is one that has been constructed by determining what is to be assessed, then the test items are administered to a sample of the population (for example, if a standardised reading test for Key Stage 2 was being constructed, the test items would be administered to a sample of pupils between the ages of 7 and 11). The results from the sample are then analysed so that norms for each age can be calculated. A standardised test is administered and scored under the same conditions so that comparisons between individuals can be made.

There are a number of basic concepts involved in norm-referenced and standardised assessment that it is important for you to understand. These are summarised below.

Table 8.1 Definitions of key terms in statistics

Term/concept	Definition
Raw score	The number of correct responses to test items. Raw scores are not used for comparisons but are converted to other scores such as standardised scores (see below).
Standardised score	A mathematical transformation of a raw score that enables comparisons between individuals to be made. A standardised score shows the difference between the individual test-taker's score and that of the mean of the group used for standardisation. A standardised score of 100 represents average attainment.
Percentile	Another way of transforming raw scores in order to make comparisons. A percentile shows the number of individuals who gained scores below a particular score. A percentile score is like giving marks out of 100, so a percentile rank of 50 represents average attainment.
Mean	A mean is obtained when all scores are added together and divided by the number of items.
Reliability	Consistency. The same results should be achieved with repeated administration of the test.
Validity	If a test is valid, it assesses what it sets out to assess.
Standard deviation	A way of showing how scores spread out from the average

Norm-referenced assessment is related to the science of *psychometrics*. Psychometrics involves measurement of psychological processes and underlying abilities. It attempts to measure individual differences in these processes and to analyse them by using statistical tools.

One major aspect of norm-referenced assessment that is a source of controversy is that of intelligence and its measurement. It is very likely that you will come across the concept of intelligence in the course of your teaching career, so we will spend some time examining this. In fact, the notion of intelligence is hinted at in the QTS standards as 'potential'. Very often, potential is used interchangeably with the term 'intelligence', since it implies a set of underlying abilities that we construe or define as being 'intelligent'.

Historical overview of the concept of and measurement of intelligence

The study of the mind was generally the province of philosophy until the nineteenth century, when a more 'scientific' approach was taken, leading eventually to the creation of the discipline of Psychology as a distinct branch of knowledge. Early attempts to take a scientific approach hypothesised that the size of the skull determined the size of the brain, thus determining the individual's level of intelligence. These early forays into the nature of intelligence had a subtext, which was to use the findings to demonstrate that white northern European peoples (or the descendents of these peoples) were the superior race. These early approaches were called phrenology or craniology.

The beginnings of the study of individual differences

Francis Galton, a cousin of Charles Darwin, was one of the first people to study the differences between individuals and to try to devise tests in order to measure these differences. He used statistics into his interpretations of results and introduced the idea of the normal distribution curve (Galton 1883).

The normal distribution curve is a graphed representation of the way in which a range of numerical values is spread, when the same property is being measured. It is sometimes called a 'bell curve' since the shape of the graph looks like a bell. Normal distribution is an example of frequency distribution and the term 'normal' is a mathematical term. The curve is shown in Figure 8.2.

The graph shows that most scores are clustered around the mean. Approximately 68 per cent of individuals will fall within one standard deviation of the mean. Many natural phenomena, such as height or weight, show normal distribution. So, if you have been told that you are overweight or underweight, this judgement will have been made by looking at your body weight in relation to a normal distribution curve illustrating body weight. Average body weight will fall within the range of values clustered around the mean. Therefore, your weight does not have to correspond to an exact value in order for you to be told that you are of average weight, overweight or underweight.

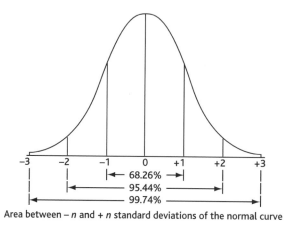

Area between – *n* and + *n* standard deviations of the normal curve

Figure 8.2   The normal distribution

Applying normal distribution to the concept of intelligence is rather more problematic. An IQ test will be standardised so that the range of scores is normally distributed. However, this does not necessarily mean that intelligence is normally distributed; only that the test has been constructed in such a way that it reflects this curve. This point is made well by Garrett (1966 : 96):

> the psychologist usually constructs his tests with the normal hypothesis definitely in mind. The resulting symmetrical distribution is to be taken, then, as evidence of the success of his efforts rather than as conclusive proof of the 'normality' of the trait being measured.

The main message here, therefore, is to treat with caution any claims that intelligence is a natural phenomenon that is normally distributed.

Although Galton's methods were far more scientifically acceptable than those made previously, he nevertheless shared the views of earlier practitioners about racial superiority and inferiority. Galton's work sparked an interest in notions of race and intelligence, leading to the formation of the *eugenics* movement. Eugenics believes that intelligence is inherited and that selective breeding can create a more intelligent population. It also subscribes to views about the relationship between intelligence and racial superiority or inferiority. The relationship between intelligence theories and eugenics is not just an interesting historical diversion. As recently as the 1990s, Herrnstein and Murray (1994) published their book *The Bell Curve: Intelligence and Class Structure in American Life*, where they suggested that there were racial differences in IQ.

The development of intelligence testing

A historical overview also needs to give a brief account of the development of intelligence testing, since this developed from Galton's early work on the measurement of individual differences. The first significant psychologist to emerge after Galton was Alfred Binet. In 1904, the French government commissioned him to develop a way of finding out whether pupils needed some form of special education. Together with Theodore Simon, he developed a series of tests that were age-related; that is, each test had different levels according to what was believed to be the 'average' performance for a given age. This test was known as the Binet-Simon Scale (Binet and Simon 1916). Binet's test was used by an American psychologist, Lewis Terman, who made changes to the tests in order to make them suitable for American children. Terman was the first to use the term IQ (Intelligence Quotient), and to develop a formula in order to calculate IQ from test scores (Terman 1916). Interestingly, Terman was a member of the eugenics movement. The test that Terman developed evolved into the Stanford-Binet intelligence test (Stanford being the university where Terman worked), and a version of this test is still available today. Despite being regarded as the 'father' of intelligence testing, Binet did not believe that intelligence was fixed and was sceptical about its measurement. He did not intend that his test should be used for ranking pupils.

The First World War was a context for further developments in intelligence testing, particularly in the USA, through the work of Yerkes. He developed a group intelligence test as an aid to the selection of recruits for the US army. The increased use of these tests meant that they were used more widely in industry and education after the war.

Further developments in intelligence testing were made by Charles Spearman (1904). Spearman developed means of applying statistical analysis to intelligence test scores. He used factor analysis in order to analyse test scores. As a result of his analyses, he proposed the notion of 'g', or a general intelligence factor. Spearman did not give a precise description or definition of g, but said that it related to 'mental energy'. 'G' was thought to be a kind of underlying ability. Spearman's factor analyses of test scores led him to propose a second aspect of intelligence, which he called 's'. This factor was related to specific abilities that assist the individual to perform in particular types of tests (for example, a test requiring verbal reasoning skills).

Two interesting facts about Spearman are worth mentioning: he was a statistician rather than a psychologist and he was a member of the eugenics movement.

The emergence of psychometrics

Spearman's work was the foundation for the science of *psychometrics*. Psychometric theories of intelligence propose that it consists of a series, or composite, of abilities that can be measured. This view of intelligence developed from the early scientists of the nineteenth century, who emphasised the heritability of intelligence. The notion of heritability led to the idea that it was fixed and could therefore be measured.

The psychometric view of intelligence dominated psychological thinking for a major part of the twentieth century. Further developments in ideas about intelligence have proposed different factors or abilities that constitute intelligence. For example, L. L Thurstone (1938) suggested seven 'primary mental abilities'. Raymond Cattell (1963) suggested two main types of intelligence: *fluid* and *crystallised*. Fluid intelligence refers to general abilities (for example reasoning skills) and crystallised intelligence refers to abilities in specific areas (general knowledge is an example of crystallised intelligence). Guilford (1967) suggested that there were up to 150 abilities involved in intelligence.

Challenging notions about intelligence

So far, the historical overview has assumed that intelligence is something that exists and can be measured. However, there is considerable debate about the concept of intelligence. For example, Howe (1990) questions whether intelligence exists, making a distinction between the use of the term as a label and as an explanation that implies a cause-and-effect relationship. A psychometric view of intelligence, based on notions of heritability, would view intelligence as an innate capacity. This may be true. However, when we begin to find ways of measuring this capacity, how do we divorce this from the individual's experience and prior learning? It would seem unrealistic to assume that the learner brings *nothing* to the testing situation. The innate ability view also implies limits, which Howe warns is a danger in an educational context: Should we suggest that there are limits to what a child can learn? Eysenck (1987) attempted a middle course, by suggesting that intelligence is subject to biological predisposition but that social and environmental factors also play a part.

It is important to appreciate that use of words such as 'intelligence' or 'potential', that form part of everyday language, is by no means indicative of a universally agreed concept. Furnham (2000) points out that the subject of intelligence is of interest to both lay and professional people, but that there are different constructions of what might constitute intelligence.

There are many criticisms of intelligence testing. For example, Elliott (2000) offers four such criticisms:

- it is not related to instruction;
- it tests products, not processes;
- there is bias built in to the tests; and
- it does not tell us how pupils learn, or fail to learn.

This last criticism is of increasing importance in relation to assessment. The government agenda for children with special educational needs is firmly rooted in inclusion. It is questionable, therefore, whether a 'technology' of assessment based on classification has any merit within this inclusive agenda.

A major criticism of the psychometric approach is that it does not take account of cultural differences. Minority ethnic groups are over-represented in special education; therefore a high level of caution and sensitivity is required when selecting and using any kind of standardised or norm-referenced instrument with diverse populations. The notion of a cultural construction of intelligence will be discussed in more detail in the next section (alternative models and theories).

The influence of the psychometric approach to intelligence can still be seen in the twenty-first century. Tests are still published that aim to measure intelligence and produce an IQ score. The Wechsler Intelligence Scale was originally developed in the 1930s by David Wechsler, a pupil of Charles Spearman (Wechsler 1939). He defined intelligence as follows: 'the global capacity of a person to act purposefully, to think rationally and to deal effectively with his/her environment'. The British Ability Scale (Elliot 1997) is based on Spearman's notion of g which it defines as: 'psychometric g is the general ability of an individual to perform complex mental processing that involves conceptualisation and the transformation of information'.

This section has shown the way in which the very earliest attempts to measure individual differences have been developed into a science in their own right, whose influence is felt up to the present day. Some criticisms of the psychometric model have been highlighted. Having read this section, use the reflection point below to consider where you stand in relation to issues about intelligence and its measurement.

REFLECTION POINT

The intelligence debate

Having read this section about intelligence, here are a few questions for you to reflect on:

How can you determine a pupil's potential?

How can you say for sure that a pupil has or has not reached their potential? Have you reached your potential?

The father of one of the authors obtained a 2.1 degree in history at the age of 78, having left school at 14. What does this tell us about potential?

If you were told a pupil's IQ, how would this help you to know what or how to teach him or her in the future?

You will probably hear the comment 's/he's really bright'. What do you think this means?

Alternative theories and models of intelligence

'It's not that I'm so smart, it's just that I stay with problems longer.' (Albert Einstein)

This quote gives a starting point for highlighting the shortcomings of a psychometric view of intelligence. Whatever one's view about underlying ability or abilities, the theory does not take account of other aspects of human behaviour that are not measured in a psychometric model. David Wechsler was aware that there was more to intelligence than a set of scores from a variety of subtests:

> While the intellectual abilities represented in this scale may be essential as precursors of intelligent behaviour, other determinants of intelligence, non-intellectual in nature, also help to determine how a child's abilities are expressed. These factors, which are not so much skills as traits and attitudes, are not directly tapped by standardised measures of intellectual ability, yet they influence a child's performance on these measures as well as his or her effectiveness in daily living and life's wider challenges. (Wechsler 1992).

In other words, there are other aspects of functioning that will affect an individual's performance in an intelligence test, but these are not measured or taken account of by the test. The quotes from Einstein and Wechsler suggest that intelligence might also have something to do with persistence. Other types of behaviour might be the way in which the individual copes with challenges, since typical practice in psychometric testing is to take the individual to failure point. What effect might this have as a test progresses?

Another omission in a psychometric theory is the impact of culture. In recent years there has been increased interest in cultural and contextual models of psychology. In relation to intelligence, a cultural model would emphasise that intelligence can only be defined in relation to what is valued by the particular culture. For example, Carraher *et al.* (1985) studied the mathematical abilities of Brazilian street children. These children had to make money in order to survive, and so developed mathematical skills. However, the street children failed when tested with conventional paper-and-pencil maths tests. Similar work, contrasting cultural and 'formal' knowledge, has been carried out in Kenya (see, for example, Sternberg and Grigorenko 1997).

Alternative theories of intelligence have arisen in response to questioning the range of abilities that intelligence tests set out to measure. These theories have as their foundation the idea that there is more to intelligence than the content of intelligence tests. Two theories will be examined: Sternberg's triarchic theory of intelligence and Gardner's theory of multiple intelligence.

Sternberg: triarchic theory

As a child Sternberg experienced test anxiety which has sparked a lifelong interest in intelligence and its measurement. He studies the processes that individuals use when solving items from IQ tests (specifically, problems involving analogies). His ideas about intelligence come from an information-processing model that also emphasises meaningful learning. Sternberg also takes the view that intelligence can be measured but that it can also be developed. His principal theory is that of triarchic intelligence (Sternberg 1985); that is, that intelligence is made up of three factors, or elements:

- Analytical intelligence: relating to problem-solving, comparing and analysing;
- Creative intelligence: relating to inventing and discovering, thinking in new or different ways; and
- Practical intelligence: relating to problem-solving in everyday contexts, adapting to the environment.

In Sternberg's view, intelligence is about adaptation to the environment. He suggests that practical intelligence is often ignored but is an important factor in intelligent behaviour.

Gardner: multiple intelligence

Howard Gardner's theory of intelligence suggests that there are multiple intelligences (Gardner 1983). He defines intelligence as 'the capacity to solve problems or to fashion products that are valued in one or more cultural setting' (Gardner and Hatch 1989). Here there is a link with Feurstein and Sternberg, through the emphasis on culture. Gardner proposes seven different types of intelligence:

- Linguistic: language and literacy;
- Logical-mathematical: logical reasoning, deduction and mathematical abilities;
- Spatial: orientation in space, directions;
- Musical: all aspects of musical ability;
- Bodily-kinaesthetic: movement and co-ordination;
- Interpersonal: understanding and relating to others; and
- Intrapersonal: understanding oneself.

In addition to the above list of seven, there have been suggestions that there are other types of intelligence, such as spiritual intelligence.

Gardner suggests that different culture values different intelligences. He also suggests that these intelligences are not separate but can work together when an individual is solving a problem. Teaching, according to Gardner, is enhanced (and is consequently more effective) when it pays attention to all of the types of intelligence, rather than a limited range (Gardner suggests that, western education typically focuses on linguistic and mathematical intelligence) and when it teaches to the individual's preferred intelligence. In Gardner's model, labelling of pupils is a result of a narrow focus on intelligence and a lack of recognition of the range of intelligences that pupils can demonstrate. In addition to the influence of his theory on teaching, Gardner suggests that assessment should measure the various forms of intelligence.

> ## THEORY AND PRACTICE LINKS
>
> **Multiple intelligences application assignment**
>
> Choose a lesson plan for a lesson you will be teaching in the near future.
>
> Using Gardner's list of seven types of intelligence, annotate your lesson plan to indicate which of the seven would be covered in the course of the lesson and which are not covered.
>
> Add some additional aspects to the lesson in order to cover at least one of the seven that is missing from your original plan.
>
> If you teach more than one subject to pupils, think about which subjects are more likely to promote particular 'intelligences'.

Concluding reflections about the intelligence debate: implications for the classroom

This part of the chapter has taken a critical look at notions of intelligence and the links between ideas about intelligence and its measurement and the eugenics movement. We have also considered two alternative theories of intelligence that attempt to take account of the role of culture and seek to broaden the notion of intelligent behaviour. In addition, suggestions about assessment and measurement seek to account for a wider range of behaviours that might affect the individual's performance. In contrast to psychometric theories, these models see intelligence as being a range of factors that are not necessarily static.

In terms of implications for the classroom, it is very important that you are clear about the words that are used when discussing pupils' progress or describing their levels of achievement. You need to think carefully about your views of 'innate abilities', since your standpoint might influence the way in which you treat children. There are significant equal-opportunity issues involved in the use of norm-referenced tests. Many tests are not standardised for use with particular groups (for example, children learning English as an additional language, children with a particular disability such as hearing impairment). Despite this fact, these tests are often used with minority groups, and decisions are made using the test results.

What can you do in order to address equal opportunity issues in relation to testing? You might not be in a position to change school policy, but you can use your knowledge to take a critical look at any tests being used so that you can feed back information to the decision makers. The box below gives some questions to consider if you are going to use norm-referenced assessments.

> ## CONSIDERATIONS TO BE MADE WHEN USING NORM-REFERENCED ASSESSMENT
>
> **What is the purpose of your assessment?** If you want to make comparisons between pupils, then a norm-referenced assessment might be useful. If you want to track progress over time (for example, whether reading ages increased over the past term?), then, again, a norm-referenced assessment might be useful. If you want to find out what to teach next it probably won't help you to use a norm-referenced test.
>
> **Who will be taking the test?** Look at the standardisation data for the test(s) you are proposing to use. How big was the sample? Is the sample representative of the pupils that you will be testing? Do your pupils fall within the recommended age range for the test?
>
> **Is the test reliable?** Look at the test development data to make sure that the test developers have made sure that results obtained will be consistent.
>
> **Is the test valid?** Does it test what you want to assess?

Types of assessment 2: criterion-referenced assessment

Criterion-referenced assessment compares a pupil's performance against a set of predetermined criteria or learning objectives. In contrast to norm-referenced assessment, it does not make comparisons between pupils. Therefore, this type of assessment can be viewed as being fairer to pupils and avoiding some of the pitfalls of norm-referenced assessment that occur when inappropriate comparisons are made (for example, using a standardised test with pupils learning English as an additional language when the test has not been standardised on EAL pupils). Criterion-referenced assessment can be of more use to teachers since it can help to identify the next steps of learning.

Criterion-referenced assessment is derived from the behavioural school of psychology. Skinner expanded the scope of his operant conditioning theory to include approaches to human learning. He developed the notion of 'programmed instruction', where questions (stimuli) and answers (responses) were organised in a series of graded steps (Skinner 1968).

A further development of Skinner's programmed instruction was the development of the concept of mastery learning. This model of learning shows its behavioural roots as it rejects any notion that learning failure is located within the learner. This contrasts with the underlying principle of norm-referenced assessment, where the focus is on assessing the learner's underlying abilities. Therefore, failure to learn is attributed to deficiencies in these underlying abilities.

In a mastery learning model, what is to be learned is specified clearly with predetermined criteria for mastery. This is where criterion-referenced assessment is used. Robert Mager (1975) was an influential individual in the development of criterion-referenced assessment in relation to mastery learning. Mager suggested a sequence of teaching and assessment: identify what is to be learned; specify the outcomes; specify how the outcomes are to be evaluated (that is, set criteria); then test the outcomes.

Effective criterion-referenced assessment is dependent on the quality of the learning objectives set. If the criteria are vague or ambiguous, it will be very difficult to determine whether they have been met. In order to ensure that criteria are useful, it is suggested that behavioural objectives are used to write criteria.

Behavioural objectives, as their name suggests, come from the school of behavioural psychology. In behavioural psychology the emphasis is on the observable. This fundamental concept is used when writing a behavioural objective. A behavioural objective has three parts:

- Action(s)
- Conditions
- Success criteria.

The action part of a behavioural objective should be a verb that represents an observable action; so descriptions such as 'read aloud' and 'write' are the kind of actions that are useful. Verbs such as 'understand' or 'appreciate' are not useful since they are not observable actions.

The conditions specify how and where learning should take place. For example, if pupils are being asked to read aloud, the conditions would specify whether this action is from a book or from flashcards.

The success criteria specify the level of acceptable performance to be achieved before the pupil can move on to the next step of learning. Here you need to decide whether one correct performance of the desired skill is acceptable. Generally, you would want the pupil to perform the skill correctly more than once if you are to be confident that it has been mastered.

Here are some examples of behavioural objectives:

- Joseph will read aloud ten high-frequency sight words from flashcards, reading all ten correctly on four separate occasions.
- Meena will write the chemical formula for elements from the Periodic Table when the names of the elements are dictated. All formulae to be written correctly on five separate occasions.
- Sharon will write the answers to 20 addition and subtraction sums, where the totals do not exceed ten. The sums are presented in random order on a sheet of A4 paper. Sharon has to complete 18 out of 20 sums correctly in one minute on three separate occasions.

Now complete the application assignment below where you are asked to write some behavioural objectives relevant to your teaching.

One example of criterion-referenced assessment can be found in the Assessment-Through-Teaching (ATT) model (Glaser 1962). ATT is a continuous cycle of assessment, teaching and evaluation. This cycle is illustrated in Figure 8.3.

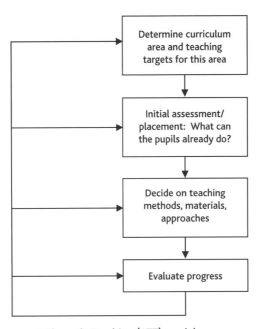

Figure 8.3 The Assessment-Through-Teaching (ATT) model

The ATT model is interesting in the light of the DfES focus on Assessment for Learning (AFL). There are similarities between the ATT model and AFL, particularly in the notion of links between assessment and future learning. Although there are other aspects of AFL that do not feature in ATT (such as the element of pupil and peer assessment), it would appear to draw its basic purpose from a model of assessment that has been around since the 1960s.

THEORY AND PRACTICE LINKS

Applying the ATT model

Use your medium- or long-term planning for this activity.

From your plan, select a curriculum focus and aspect of the curriculum that you are going to teach. Use the ATT model to plan and evaluate your teaching. Here are some points to help you:

- The initial assessment can be something that you devise yourself. If you do this, use behavioural objectives, as it will then be easy to tell whether progress has been made. You could use the objectives you drew up in the exercise contained previously.

- If you don't start from scratch in devising an initial assessment, you can use a ready-made diagnostic test, or something like a word list from the National Literacy Strategy.

- Use the information from the initial assessment to plan the next steps of teaching and decide how you are going to teach.

- Decide on the length of time that you will carry out your teaching. There is no hard-and-fast rule: you might want to evaluate after a few days, or a week. Don't continue the teaching for too long, though, because the purpose of using ATT is to evaluate and then make changes if necessary. It's a bit late to do this if your teaching programme lasts a whole term.

Re-administer your assessment. Look at the results and decide which part of the model you have to go back to. If the pupil has achieved the set goals, then you will move on to another set of teaching targets. If not, you have to think about where in the cycle you need to make changes.

Summary

This chapter has examined a core function of teaching, that of assessment. We have considered contributions from cognitive and behavioural psychology as part of an examination of two major types of assessment. In particular, we have cast a fairly critical eye over the concept of intelligence and the notion of what is meant by potential. This in-depth coverage of the intelligence debate is thought to be necessary since there are many parents and educators who use the terms 'intelligence' and 'potential' without much thought as to their meaning. Sadly, many educational psychologists still use IQ tests as their main method of assessment, despite a great deal of disquiet within the profession about the validity and usefulness of such a procedure. It is hoped that the information in this chapter should help you to carry out effective assessment that informs teaching and does not merely serve to label or classify pupils.

CHAPTER 9

Understanding and managing special educational needs

Introduction and chapter aims

> If I had to reduce all of educational psychology to just one principle, I would say this: the most important single factor influencing learning is what the learner already knows. Ascertain this and teach him accordingly. (Ausabel 1968: 18)

A child has special educational needs if they have a learning difficulty which calls for special educational provision to be made for them.

A child has a learning difficulty if they:

a have a significantly greater difficulty in learning than the majority of children the same age; or

b have a disability which prevents or hinders the child from making use of educational facilities of a kind generally provided for children of the same age within the area of the local education authority

c is under five and falls within the definition at (a) or (b) above or would so do if special educational provision was not made for that child.

A child must not be regarded as having a learning difficulty solely because the language or medium of communication of the home is different from the language in which he or she will be taught.

(Education Act 1996, Section 312)

This chapter aims to:

- provide a brief historical perspective of special needs;
- describe two different models of disability;
- consider the psychology of attribution and labelling;
- describe the application of behavioural psychology to developing special programmes using task and skills analyses;
- describe the processes of differentiation within the curriculum;

- outline the concepts of 'gifted and talented' and their uses in education; and
- examine the concept of 'special needs' in an international context.

Brief history

If there has been a broad trend over time it has been that of increasing inclusion of people in education. A thousand years ago, education was the province of religious orders who considered their duties to be the promotion of religious beliefs. Knowledge of Latin and Greek was a high priority. Children with disabilities or differences were not high priorities. It was not until the eighteenth century that education was considered either possible or desirable for deaf or blind children. The mid-nineteenth century saw development of provision for the 'mentally handicapped' and 'physically disabled'. When the 1870 Education Act established compulsory schooling for all, special classes were created for children with 'sensory and physical handicaps'. At the end of the century the committee on 'Defective and Epileptic' children recommended access to education for this group.

At the beginning of the twentieth century, Binet and Simon developed tests to determine the *mental age* of children. This was used to help plan educational programmes for children with some kind of educational difficulty. Maria Montessori opened her first school in 1907 in which she developed programmes for children described as *defective* or *ineducable*. In 1944, education became compulsory for all until age 14, with 11 groups or *categories* of children (including a group defined as *severely sub-normal*, and cared for by the health, rather than education, services). This continued until 1970 when this group was included in education with the term *educationally sub-normal (severe)*. These categories defined segregated education in special schools. The processes underpinning these educational arrangements derived from a *medical model* of diversity in children. This can be visualised as shown in Figure 9.1.

By the mid-1970s this approach was being challenged. In Italy many well-educated parents of children defined as *handicapped* took their children away from the hospital or special schools out of dissatisfaction with the quality of education they were receiving. The Italian government then took the radical move of closing all the special schools and placing the children in local mainstream provision. Teams developed around the children including specialist teachers, psychologists, therapists and care assistants. This model is still in use after 30 years. Although practitioners criticise the speed of the change and the lack of preparation for the new children, there is no enthusiasm for a return to the old system. Social inclusion is seen as very positive.

In the UK, the Warnock Report (1978) changed the approach and thinking about education of children with differences. Categories were removed and the concept of a *special educational need* was introduced. Statements of need and the

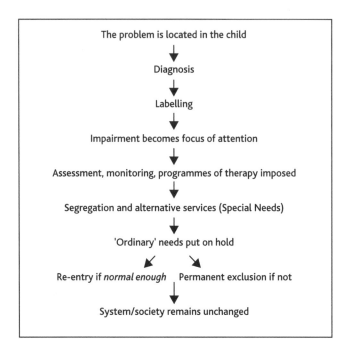

Figure 9.1   The medical model of disability

involvement of parents were introduced. *Integration* was the term used to encourage children to be educated in local mainstream schools. This led to *inclusion* being the philosophy behind special education. By 1998 there were green and white

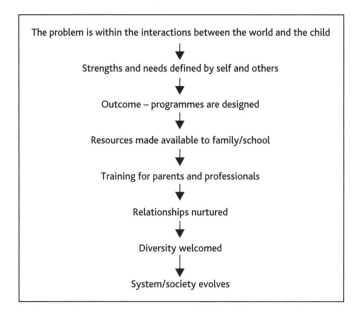

Figure 9.2   The social care model of disability

papers calling for 'inclusion of all', and in 2002 the Disability Discrimination Act applied to all schools and it became an offence to discriminate against children with special educational needs in all schools. The medical model gave way to the *social model* of diversity (Figure 9.2):

Although not universally supported, this is the more contemporary model.

Let us illustrate this with a case study:

CASE STUDY

Shaun is nine years old. He has had a complicated life with many changes of school arising from difficulties between his parents. He now lives with his father. He is very interested in bicycles and spends a lot of time tinkering with, adapting and riding his mountain bike. He likes computer games and when he is not playing with his bike, he is playing on the play station. He never liked sitting and reading and his teachers have said that his reading is about the same as that of an average six-year-old. At school he is impatient in class and gets into trouble for not sitting still, especially in literacy. He is competent orally and answers questions when interested.

Application of the medical model

Shaun is found to have poor literacy, yet good other skills. This leads to a diagnosis of dyslexia. There is a centre for dyslexia where many children with these difficulties attend. It is a unit attached to a school on the outskirts of town. Shaun is sent there, where emphasis is on teaching him to read and spell. Other programmes are available, as dyslexic pupils often have difficulty with balance and co-ordination. (Shaun does not; he has practised on his mountain bike.) Shaun's reading is measured, and if it accelerates, so that it becomes closer to those of the other pupils, he will return. Typically, this takes at least two years, although some pupils never 'catch up'.

Application of the social model

Shaun, his father and teachers all agree that learning to read is a good idea; however, his *access* to the rest of the curriculum must not be limited by his poor literary skills. The school *differentiates* his educational programme in three ways:

1   He is allowed to access written text in class by having it read to him.

2   Where he is required to express himself by writing, he can dictate it to an assistant, who writes it down. He then copies it into his own book.

3   He is given a special reading programme which starts at the point he got to. This is used both at school and at home.

Application of medical and social models

Consider a child you know who has some kind of diversity. Work though the medical and social models described above. What differences in approach do they suggest? If you were that child, what would be the advantages and disadvantages of each model?

Psychological aspects of labelling and attribution

One of the advantages of the social model is that it changes the nature of *attribution*. Consider the following argument:

> Neelam can't read even simple words at the age of nine; therefore Neelam must be dyslexic.

> How do you know that Neelam is dyslexic?

> Because she can't read at the age of nine.

We call this the *explanatory fiction*. The *attribution* of Neelam's lack of reading is a hypothesised condition. However, it does nothing to advance the understanding of the problem. In fact, it probably makes it worse. This has been the subject of study in psychology.

Jones *et al.* (1979) created an experimental paradigm to look at attribution. The subjects listened to tape recordings of other students reading essays about racial segregation. Two elements were varied, the attitude towards segregation (for or against) and the degree to which the 'authors' had *choice* about whether to write a pro- or anti-segregation essay. (In fact, the experimenters provided the scripts.) The experimental subjects were asked to indicate whether the 'authors' were, in fact, pro- or anti-segregation. As expected, when the subjects believed that the authors were able to choose the stance, they inferred that the attitudes expressed in the essay were actually those held by those authors. However, they also inferred that the authors held the views expressed for the group they believed had been told the stance to write about. In other words, the subjects tended to ignore the *situational* factors influencing the behaviour of the supposed authors. This finding has been replicated by many other studies.

This has been extended to cover the differences in attribution between observers and participants. Studies by Nisbett *et al.* (1973) demonstrated convincingly that observers are likely to attribute the behaviour of a person in terms of personality, disposition or person-centred qualities, rather than situational ones, whereas the person concerned is more likely to attribute their own behaviour in terms of the situation, or environmental factors external to themselves. This is commonplace in classrooms. Teachers will attribute actions to children, who, in turn, will attribute the actions externally. Typically, 'It wasn't me miss, it was them. They made me do it/started it . . .'.

Let us apply this to the labelling of special educational needs. A child may not be reading fluently by the age of nine. The tendency is to attribute this in terms of the disposition of the child, or some variable inside the child. The child may attribute this differently: 'It's boring', or 'It's hard', or 'No-one helped me'. However, if the child begins to agree with the internal attribution, he/she may internalise a high degree of helplessness: 'I can't read very well because my brain doesn't work properly – I was born like this'.

Helplessness has been explored, again experimentally. Seligman (1975) devised experiments with dogs and rats. Dogs were placed in situations in which they were unable to avoid some electric shocks. They appeared to give up and just accept the shocks. When they were subsequently placed in situations in which they *could* avoid the shocks, they did not do so, whereas other dogs who had only been placed in the second situation quickly learned to avoid the shocks. He used the term *learned helplessness* to describe the behaviour of the first set of animals.

Helplessness has been linked to depression. Although a comprehensive analysis of depression is beyond the scope of this book. People suffering from unipolar depression tend to feel helpless and attribute problems in ways beyond their influence. This insight has been applied very positively to the management of care homes for the elderly. Langer and Rodin (1976) looked at the messages conveyed at the beginning of a stay in a nursing home. If the messages induced responsibility in the clients, they reported higher degrees of happiness and activity. These findings persisted and the group given responsibility lived longer. In other words, both quality and length of life were enhanced if the people felt empowered and in control of their lives.

If we apply these principles to Neelam we begin to see the dangers of labelling. If Neelam believes that the reason she is finding reading difficult is that she finds it boring or that no-one has taught her properly, there exists the possibility of change. If, however, she attributes it to a constitutional or innate property of herself, there is no possibility of change. 'Why bother to try? It's no use, because I'm dyslexic.' Many children have said to teachers, 'It's no use trying to teach me to read, I'm dyslexic'.

The social model of special needs emphasises the *need* rather than the *condition*, thus *externalising* the cause and creating the idea that situations can change, thereby empowering the change itself.

CASE STUDY

The following is a case known to the authors.

A 12-year-old girl was referred to the educational psychology service after she had slashed her wrists. Her basic skills were poor. Her reading was at the level of the average seven- or eight-year-old. However, she was extremely talented at athletics and showed considerable promise in a number of areas. The psychologist explored her attribution of her poor literacy. She had been told by her mother that she must be dyslexic and that, therefore, she would always find reading difficult. She enjoyed her sport and wanted to become a coach, but knew that she had to pass GCSEs, including English. She believed that her 'dyslexia' would prevent her from doing that and she could not see a future. The psychologist analysed her reading and used precision teaching to demonstrate that she could make progress. He suggested that she had probably been badly taught and that her brain was perfectly capable of learning how to read; therefore she was probably not 'dyslexic' in the sense her mother meant. The girl went on to learn to read and was accepted for a national squad in her chosen field. She did pass her GCSE and was able to embark on a course leading to her chosen career.

THEORY AND PRACTICE LINK

Attribution of success

Consider something that you are good at and something you are not so good at. To what do you attribute your success and lack of it? If possible, ask someone who knows you to speculate on this success and lack of success. What are the differences?

Use of behavioural theory

If we return to the definition of Special Educational Needs found in the Code of Practice we find the centrality of the *difficulty* in learning. The assessment of difficulty will usually be made by looking at levels of attainment. Low attainment usually defines special need. Behavioural psychology offers a model for defining special need in terms of the curriculum and ways of meeting that need by modified or *differentiated* programmes of study. The concepts central to this model are:

- skills analysis; and
- task analysis.

Skills analysis

Children acquire skills through interactions with the environment. For this purpose the environment includes parents, adults, teachers, television and other children. We can analyse the skills that children have by looking at different skill areas. There are various ways of categorising skills, but one currently used by the DfES is the Foundation Stage profile:

- Personal, social and emotional development.
- Communication, language and literacy.
- Mathematical development.
- Knowledge and understanding of the world.
- Physical development.
- Creative development.

Within each area, skills are organised in order of complexity. If we consider Physical Development we see:

1 Moves spontaneously, showing some control and co-ordination.

2 Moves with confidence in a variety of ways, showing some awareness of space.

3 Usually shows appropriate control in large- and small-scale movements.

4 Moves with confidence, imagination and in safety. Travels around, under, over and through balancing and climbing equipment. Shows awareness of space, of self and others.

5 Demonstrates fine motor control and co-ordination.

6 Uses small and large equipment, showing a range of basic skills.

7 Handles tools, objects, construction and malleable materials safely and with basic control.

8 Recognises the importance of keeping healthy and those things which contribute to this. Recognises the changes that happen to her/his body when s/he is active.

There are more-finely graded skills analyses which tend to be used to define areas of difficulty in children with more complex skills profiles, but the principles behind their use remain the same. Skills have different degrees of complexity and we expect children to acquire simple skills before more complex ones.

The task at this stage is to build up a picture of the skills that the child can demonstrate. This can be achieved by a combination of simple observation and individual testing. If children are being assessed, good practice would be to do this over a period of time so that the child becomes accustomed to the situation in which the task is presented. See Chapter 8 for more information about this. Once the profile of skills is built up, the second aspect is to examine the tasks provided for the child in the classroom.

Task analysis

Classroom life can be considered as a sequence of tasks that the teacher requires the pupil to perform. Sometimes they may be as simple as sitting and listening to the teacher and answering questions at the end. Others may involve more complex sequences. Analysing the tasks involves looking at both *sequence* of activities and the *skills* required to complete the tasks. Let us start with an example:

Teacher instruction: 'On your whiteboards write down as many ways as you can of making 10. Think about your number bonds.'

First analysis is *sequence*:

Activity 1: Listen to teacher instruction.
Activity 2: Identify location of whiteboard.
Activity 3: Place whiteboard in writing position.
Activity 4: Find marker pen.
Activity 5: Hold marker pen.
Activity 6: Write down number less than 10.
Activity 7: Subtract this number from 10.
Activity 8: Write number on white board in form A + B =10.
Activity 9: Repeat activities 5 to 8 until told to stop.

However, the next analysis looks at prerequisite skills. Take Activity 5 and consider the following:

To write down a number less than 10 you need to be able to write numbers 0–10; which in turn requires you to be able to identify numbers 0–10; which in turn requires you to be able to sequence numbers 0–10; which in turn requires you to be able to demonstrate knowledge of 'less than'; which in turn requires you to be able to count on from a given number less than 10; which in turn requires you to be able to count from 0 to 10.

We could go further and look at speech, but let us stop here for this item. Each of the elements of the task can be analysed in depth. This analysis of the task(s) is then compared with the analysis of skills possessed by the child. Differences and gaps are looked for. So any *special need* is set in the context of the task rather than some deficit that the child may be perceived to have.

Practical example of task and skills analysis

A useful process which brings both analyses together is an *informal reading inventory*. By listening to a child read text we can establish the percentage of words the child gets right: more than 95 per cent accuracy is suitable for *independent* reading. The child can probably access the text without the need for assistance.

Between 90 and 95 per cent accuracy is suitable for *supported* reading. The child will need someone to assist. This is the band most suitable for teaching reading. It is known as *instructional* as it maximises opportunities for children to correct themselves. Note, though, that the term *instructional* refers to the teaching of reading rather than the use of text for instruction of other subjects.

Less than 90 per cent accuracy is known as *frustrational*. The meaning of the text is lost as the error rate is too high to fill in the gaps.

This method combines the skills analysis and task analysis in a single operation. Establishing that the text is appropriate for either independent or instructional purposes ensures a match between the skills and the task.

> **THEORY AND PRACTICE LINK**
>
> **Practical application**
>
> Take a child in a class who appears to be struggling with some element of the curriculum. Take a typical piece of text that the child needs to access. This could be a worksheet, book or even words on a whiteboard. Ask the child to read this aloud and establish at what level the text is (independent/instructional/frustrational). If the child is not reading the text at an independent level, are there different ways in which the child can be given the information?

Differentiation

Historically, special needs were met in alternative settings.

The changing of an educational arrangement for a child is called *differentiation*. There are different ways of differentiating. Benton and O'Brien (2000) look at three:

- differentiation by placement;
- differentiation by curriculum; and
- differentiation by pedagogy.

The Salamanca Statement (UNESCO 1994) strongly encourages inclusive education and supports the development of special needs programmes as an integral part of all educational programmes. It does not support differentiation by placement.

The National Curriculum is aimed at all pupils. It encourages modified (or differentiated) targets for pupils. The curriculum, however, is for all, therefore differentiation by large-scale changes to the curriculum is not encouraged.

This leaves pedagogy. As Benton and O'Brien point out, teachers routinely vary their pedagogic styles to suit children. The Assessment-Through-Teaching model described in Chapter 8 can be refined for children making slow progress:

1   Establish that the child has the prerequisite skills to access the task.

2   Define the outcome in terms that are observable.

3   Reduce the element(s) to be learned to suit the child.

4   Teach the element(s) as directly as possible on a daily basis.

5   Assess the pupil's learning at the end of the teaching cycle.

6   Assess the pupil's retention of the learning before the next teaching cycle.

7   Assess the pupil's recall of the skill in different settings.

8   Only move on to a new target when the child has attained the present one.

The differentiation comes in stages 2 and 3 by reduction or *slicing* the task into smaller elements.

If we take the example from numeracy cited earlier and focus on teaching number bonds to 10, the task may be sliced quite easily by focusing on number bonds to 5 first.

THEORY AND PRACTICE LINK

Task analysis

Take these two targets from numeracy and literacy and:

1   identify the prerequisite skills needed access the task;

2   slice the task into smaller teaching units.

Example from Numeracy:

Target from Year 3: **Order whole numbers to at least 1,000** and position them on a number line.

(The phrase in **bold** represents the key objective.)

Example from Literacy. To:

● identify phonemes in speech and writing;

● blend phonemes for reading; and

● segment words into phonemes for spelling.

Gifted and talented as additional need

Although not generally included as a *special* educational need, the issue of gifted and talented has been considered as an *additional* educational need. The concepts of gifted and talented are well embedded in educational thinking, but there is a lack of agreement on the nature, origins and wisdom of using these terms. VanTassel-Baska (1998) provides a useful historical perspective:

1880s	'Genius' used. Galton produced a book, *Heredity Genius*, in 1889.
1905	Binet's intelligence scale published leading to the term 'intellectually gifted' being applied to people who scored very highly on the tests.
1925	Terman published *Genetic Studies of Genius*.
1930s	The term 'gifted' introduced.
1942	Hollingworth published *Children Above 180 IQ*.
1950	Guilford's presidential address to the American Psychological Association proposing 120 aspects of intelligence. Concepts of convergent and divergent thinkers introduced.
1960s/1970s	Concepts of multi-talented people emerge. Conference on gifted and talented recognises intellectual, academic, creative, visual and performing arts, leadership and psychomotor abilities.
1983	Gardner publishes *Frames of Mind*, introducing concepts of multiple intelligence.
1985	Sternberg publishes *Beyond IQ*. Introduces componential theory of giftedness.
1990s	Educational programmes for 'Gifted and Talented' introduced.

So the origins of the concepts of gifted and talented come from performance on IQ tests. Although definitions vary, the following has been suggested by Gross (1993):

IQ>125	moderately gifted
IQ>145	highly gifted
IQ>160	exceptionally gifted
IQ>190	profoundly gifted

The English educational system was stimulated into using IQ tests to identify giftedness by an extensive report prepared in 1924 on 'Psychological Tests of Educable Capacity'. The authors suggest:

A high level of ability does not therefore invariably entail a good standard of school work. It has often been pointed out that many highly gifted men and women were regarded in their schools days as dull or incompetent. Such dullness or incompetence may have been generally present, owing to a failure of interest in the pupil, or to an arrested development of ability which was subsequently released. Insofar as it is the fault of the school, it may not be so much the conventional methods of teaching that are inadequate as the ordinary means of diagnosis, consisting chiefly of written, oral and practical examinations. The school should be criticised not so much for failing to adapt itself to such exceptional personalities as for failing to discover them.

(Selby-Bigge 1924)

This report was heavily influenced by Cyril Burt and represented a fundamental shift in thinking. Prior to the 1880s the attribution of the term 'genius' was based on an individual's performance in a given area. A mathematical genius was one who excelled in mathematics, a musical genius excelled in music. IQ tests became a *proxy* indicator. Because an individual performed exceptionally well on these tests they *ought* to be considered a genius irrespective of their attainments in other areas. It left the way clear for discrepancies between performance on the IQ test and performance in some skill that is generally valued.

As we saw in Chapter 8, the nature of 1Q tests is often misrepresented and their use is highly suspect. The application of these tests to identify children is not without dangers. We begin with a powerful, in-depth study by Freeman (1991).

This study was conducted over 14 years. Freeman examined three groups of children aged 5 to 14:

1   70 children identified by their parents as 'gifted'.

2   70 children matched by measures of ability, but not identified by their parents as 'gifted'.

3   70 randomly selected children.

The initial findings included that the first two groups did not present emotional or social problems, but that the first group had significantly more behaviour problems than the second group. The children were followed up ten years later and the group *labelled* as gifted (the first group) had often remained the least happy. The conclusion seems clear, the *label* led to pressure on the child rather than the high ability. In fact, the overall findings were that achievement at school was more related to access to facilities for learning and parental involvement. The author suggested that a cause of the pressure was parents feeling inadequate or trying to live their lives through their children. If problems existed in the family anyway, they tended to be expressed through the 'gifted' child.

Koren *et al.* (1992) examined the impact of labelling the top 10 per cent of pupils in Croatia as gifted based on four tests of ability. This created a group of 1,215 pupils who were given special programmes. Their findings included the view from the children that the label 'gifted' posed a danger to their personalities and created conflict with their parents over choice of school. The children did not wish to be educated separately. In China, a 15-year study of 'extremely high IQ children' revealed that parents taught the children to read very early, but that social relationships were poor and parents needed lessons to help the children socialise better (Shi and Zha 2000).

Freeman (1997) reported that labelled children can be pressurised by parents and teachers to be successful in examinations. This can lead to a reduction in access to more emotionally satisfying activities such as art, and even more intellectually challenging pursuits that don't feature in public examinations.

The evidence so far suggests that labelling has more negative consequences for the child than positive. Education, however, has an obligation to all children to maximise their development. Not tailoring the curriculum to meet the needs of highly skilled children would represent a failure.

VanTassel-Baska (1998) suggests strategies for gifted pupils:

- opening and warm-up exercises that engage students in a challenging cognitive activity;
- lectures, lecturettes, teacher presentations and explanations that present the current conceptions of fundamental ideas in the discipline and induce students to think critically and creatively;
- reading and homework that advance the students' understanding of the concepts, expose them to primary sources and enhance their self-regulatory skills;
- evoking intrinsic motivation through creating interest, relating new information to previously learned material, modelling enthusiasm for the subject material, and commending specific achievements;
- discussions, questioning and dialogue that challenge and extend the students' thinking skills and help them to incorporate new ideas into their schematic frameworks;
- small-group projects, seminars and debates that provide opportunities for in-depth and collaborative work and reinforce extemporaneous thinking skills;
- library and empirical research that illustrates the importance of problem definition and the use of the scientific reasoning processes.

The suggestions are probably as relevant for the whole school population as for children identified as gifted. The key to effective education of any group is to assess what they know already and teach them accordingly. Children who learn very quickly have the same needs as any others: a programme of study which starts from where they are and extends them at a rate which retains their interest. The key to educating both 'gifted' children and those described as having 'special needs' lies in programmes which are tailored to the individual.

Alternative perspectives

Throughout this chapter we have assumed a common understanding of what a special (or additional) educational need is. The Code of Practice describes difficulties in learning or disabilities. The majority of children now described as having special needs fall into the former category. It may seem simplistic to note that this depends on:

1 agreed definitions of what is to be learned; and

2 agreed and systematic ways of measuring what is learned.

So the historical definitions of handicap which usually related to visible medical conditions have given way to new definitions of special need which define vulnerability in terms of children who will not develop skills, usually by a certain age. Concern is focused on children who will not achieve National Curriculum level 4 by the age of (say) 11. This concept is culturally created.

Chitiyo and Wheeler (2004) have examined the nature of special educational needs in Zimbabwe. The starting point is familiar – children and adults who are not accepted in society. They comment that the lack of services for people with disabilities was not simply a product of the colonial system. People with physical or mental disabilities were not respected in society and some communities shunned them as outcasts. Of the 54,900 children identified as having some kind of disability or difference, only 6,600 were considered as a result of 'mental retardation and behaviour disorders'. The rest (nearly 90%) had medical conditions such as sensory impairment, limb disabilities or spinal disorders. In fact 14 per cent of the country was assessed as 'illiterate', so a definition of special need based on literacy would generate very large numbers of children.

European approaches to special needs

The definition of special needs, therefore, is dependent on culture. Expressed positively, it attempts to include children who were not traditionally included in education, and it affects funding.

In the UK, children with special needs usually have funding additional to that normally available for other pupils. Currently about 3 per cent of pupils in the UK have additional funding (or alternative educational placements) arising from an identified special need. There is considerable variation across Europe. The Code of Practice describes about 20 per cent of the school population as experiencing some kind of difficulty in their school careers.

The Czech Republic provides compulsory education from six to 15 years of age. Approximately 3 per cent of pupils are educated in segregated special schools. There are nine categories of disability: mental retardation, physical disability, emotional disturbance, visual impairment, hearing impairment, language disorder, learning disability, medical/health impairment, and multiple or combined disabilities.

Denmark provides compulsory education from seven to 15 years of age. Thirteen per cent of pupils are identified as requiring special education. This is provided in local mainstream (or *folkeskol*) schools. They do not define categories, but specify seven categories for placement purposes. About 11.5 per cent of pupils receive special support in ordinary classes; about 1 per cent attend special classes and about 0.65 per cent attend special schools.

Norway provides education for all children from seven to 16 years of age. Three per cent receive additional provision in mainstream schools and 0.7 per cent attend 'special educational provision'. There is no use of categories of disability.

The Netherlands has 7 per cent of pupils attending special provision. These special schools are well resourced and popular with parents. In spite of an inclusive policy at national level, it has proved difficult to move children into mainstream schools. There are seven categories of disability.

Germany provides education from age 6 to 18. Approximately 3.1 per cent of pupils are enrolled in special education. There is a general policy of inclusion. Seven categories of disability are used.

Italy established rights for disabled pupils as early as 1971 and closed special schools in the mid-1970s. The government was accused of 'wild integration' (*integrazione selvaggia*) and recklessness. About 1.8 per cent of the school population are now identified as disabled. The system has now become more organised with multi-professional teams meeting on a monthly basis to discuss the progress of identified children. Class sizes are halved if an identified child is present. There will only be one pupil per class with an identified disability and there is a support teacher for six to eight hours per week.

The concept, therefore, varies for different countries. Although there is broad agreement on identification of children with sensory and physical disabilities, the issue of attainment varies considerably. In the UK the development of the 'Every Child Matters' agenda may change the focus for central services. A *special need* may become defined in more social terms. The new domains may become:

Being healthy:
- physically
- mentally and emotionally
- sexually
- having healthy lifestyles
- choosing not to take drugs

Staying safe:

- from maltreatment, neglect, violence and sexual exploitation
- from accidental injury and death
- from bullying and discrimination
- from crime and anti-social behaviour in and out of school
- having security, stability and being cared for

Enjoying and achieving:

- ready for school
- attend and enjoy school
- achieve educational standards at primary school
- achieve personal and social development and enjoy recreation
- achieve educational standards at secondary school

Making a positive contribution:

- engage in decision-making and support the community and environment
- engage in law-abiding and positive behaviour in and out of school
- develop positive relationships and choose not to bully and discriminate
- develop self-confidence and deal successfully with significant life changes and challenges
- develop enterprising behaviour

Achieve economic well-being:

- engage in further education, employment or training on leaving school
- ready for employment
- live in decent homes and sustainable communities
- access to transport and material goods
- live in households free from financial anxieties

Those children at risk of not achieving these may become the new focus for intervention by the state. This would subtly redefine the concept of special needs. Children at risk of social exclusion through drugs, crime, poor housing and nutrition may become the new *children with special needs* rather than those whose academic progress is seen to prejudice a school's performance in some published league table of SATs or GCSE results. It remains to be seen to what extent this develops.

Summary

Children vary in their rates of learning; some learn very quickly and some much more slowly. This chapter has described some of the concepts behind changing what is taught in schools to match the needs of all children. It has outlined a methodology for matching what is taught to the needs of different children. It has presented some differences in approach found in different countries and speculated on future developments in the UK. Attaining Qualified Teacher Status will require a working knowledge of the Code of Practice for Special Educational Needs. We hope that the contents of this chapter will assist in understanding the rationale behind the Code.

CHAPTER 10

The reflective teacher

Introduction and chapter aims

Teachers lead busy professional lives. There is far more to teaching than face-to-face interactions between teachers and pupils. There are many tasks that teachers are expected to undertake as part of their professional duties which do not require direct contact with pupils but which will, nevertheless, impact on this contact. There is a lot of work that relates specifically to direct teacher and pupil contact in the classroom. But there are even more indirect matters, such as planning, knowledge of the curriculum, assessment and record keeping, to consider as well. It could be argued that this balance is about right, since the effectiveness of direct pupil–teacher contact should be related to the quality of 'behind the scenes' work that is involved in teaching. Nowadays it simply isn't enough to be a charismatic adult (although clearly the ability to relate to children and young people has to be an important aspect of teaching); reflection about practice is also important and is part of a teacher's professional development.

Becoming a reflective practitioner involves far more than just thinking about the job. It is a deliberate, active process of evaluation and goal setting that might also involve aspects of research and evidence-based practice. The aims of this chapter, therefore, are as follows:

- to help you to develop skills of reflection and evaluation in order to enhance your teaching; and
- to understand some basic principles underlying educational research and some methodologies used in educational research in order to help you to interpret and apply research and evidence-based practice in your classroom.

Psychological underpinnings of reflective practice

Our first steps in thinking about reflective practice will be to consider some psychological perspectives of adult learning. The various models of adult learning and reflective practice described below are all derived from *humanistic psychology*. The humanistic perspective can be seen as one of three major schools of thought that emerged in twentieth-century psychology, the other two being the psycho-analytic tradition and the behaviourist tradition. Humanistic psychology emerged during the second half of the twentieth century, but can trace its roots to *existentialist philosophy* which arose in the nineteenth century (the Danish philosopher Kierkegaard was the first to use the term 'existential'. An existentialist view emphasises free will and responsibility; it rejects the idea that knowledge can be objective or scientific and places importance on personal experience. Subjectivity, therefore, is the means of knowing, because objective knowledge is considered unattainable. With this broad philosophical tradition at its foundation, humanistic psychology emphasises understanding the nature of humanity. It takes the view that humans are self-determining and that we are influenced by our perceptions of ourselves. Personal growth is an important aspect of the humanistic tradition.

What is a reflective practitioner?

The QTS standards represent a balance of what we might call 'direct' and 'indirect' teaching, reflecting a very broad view of teaching: what we might call *pedagogy*, or the science of teaching. The term 'pedagogy' implies more than just teacher and pupil interaction; it encompasses all aspects of educating children and young people. The word is derived from two Greek words meaning 'child' and 'lead'.

The notion of pedagogy has been introduced in order to orientate you to the notion of the reflective teacher. We would suggest that the QTS standards represent the 'establishment' view of what constitutes pedagogy, that is, a range of areas of practice that define education and the profession of teaching. Therefore, many aspects of pedagogy are not concerned with direct pupil–teacher interactions but are concerned with the way in which those interactions will have maximum impact on pupils. Becoming a reflective practitioner is part of the development of effective pedagogy.

The term 'reflective practitioner' is easy to say but less easy to define. As we implied earlier, it is not just a case of thinking about the job. As Kuit *et al.* (2001) point out: 'in everyday conversation [reflective practice] has been devalued to describe merely thinking about a subject without the element of query and enquiry'.

The term 'reflective practitioner' was first used extensively by Donald Schön (Schön, 1983, 1987). Schön used the term 'reflection in action'. This is a process where implicit, unconscious knowledge about practice is brought to the forefront of the practitioner's mind through a process of thinking about his or her actions at the same time as those actions are being carried out. Schön also differentiated this process from what he called *reflection on action*, a process that is retrospective and involves thinking about one's actions after they have taken place.

Being a reflective practitioner, therefore, is a conscious process that involves experience and has a systematic element to it. Lucas (1991) emphasises the systematic characteristic of reflection that enhances the practitioner's understanding of their practice. Experience is also an important element, since reflection involves reviewing an experience as part of a process of description, analysis and evaluation that informs practice (Reid 1993). Day (1999) emphasises the emotional element of reflection; this is what distinguishes the process from being merely a cognitive process.

The brief overview above suggests that a reflective practitioner might be defined as an individual who uses their experiences in order to inform their practice. The purpose of this is to effect change and improvement as part of the individual's professional development.

Models of adult learning and reflective practice

Knowles: the concept of andragogy
Knowles (1984) uses the term *andragogy* (in contrast to the term *pedagogy*, which was discussed in the introduction to this chapter) to describe adult learning. He makes the distinction because he views adult learning as being different from that of children. He bases this distinction on four assumptions:

- adults are self-directive;
- experience is a source for learning;
- adults have a readiness to learn; and
- adults are orientated to learning as a problem-solving process (rather than a content-orientated process).

More recently, Knowles has suggested motivation as an additional element.

THEORY AND PRACTICE LINKS

Knowles's assumptions about adult learners

Knowles's attempt to create a separate 'science of teaching' (i.e. andragogy) was not universally accepted, because it was thought that he had not necessarily identified distinctive and separate characteristics of adults and children as learners.

Look at the assumptions by Knowles about adult learners.

Do you think they only apply to adults?

If not, think of some examples from your teaching where children have demonstrated these characteristics.

Despite the criticisms, we could agree that these are *appropriate* characteristics of learners, even if we do not think that they are *distinctive*.

As an adult learner, insight into your processes of learning will be helpful.

Look again at Knowles's assumptions. Think of a situation where you learned successfully. Which of the characteristics did you display, and how did they help you to learn successfully?

Kolb: experiential learning

David Kolb suggested the idea of *experiential learning*. This idea is used with particular reference to adult learning, although experiential learning as a broad discipline is not just about adults (see Chapter 6, where the application of an experiential approach is described in relation to classroom management). Kolb's view of experiential learning has its roots in the work of John Dewey. Dewey rejected the notion that education was simply the transmission of knowledge; he proposed that knowledge is a means to an end, not the end itself (Dewey 1938).

In Kolb's model, learning is represented as a cycle, as illustrated in Figure 10.1

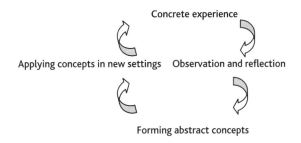

Concrete experience

Applying concepts in new settings   Observation and reflection

Forming abstract concepts

Figure 10.1   Kolb's Learning Cycle

Each stage of the cycle can be described further, as follows:

- *Concrete experience:* this is just what it says, an experience or specific action that is the usual starting point for the cycle;
- *Observation and reflection:* this is where the individual thinks about the effect or outcome of the action/experience;
- *Forming abstract concepts:* after observing and reflecting, the individual might then generate a principle or set of principles. Kolb uses Piaget's term assimilation to describe the process at this point of the cycle; and
- *Applying concepts in new settings:* having derived principles, these can then be used in different settings and contexts.

AN EXAMPLE OF KOLB'S EXPERIENTIAL LEARNING CYCLE

Concrete experience
Today I introduced a new letter sound to my class. When I reviewed what we had covered at the end of the lesson, half of the class could say the correct sound when I showed them the letter.

Observation and reflection
I thought that more children would have been able to make the letter/sound association by the end of the lesson.

I think I should have provided a wider range of practice activities, not just worksheets.

The children might have been sitting and listening for too long, because they were very restless at the end of the lesson.

Forming abstract concepts
Learning takes place more effectively when plenary sessions are fairly short and when there are many opportunities for practice.

Applying concepts in new settings
When I introduce something new in maths, I will have a short plenary session and finish it before the children become restless. I will have lots of practice activities that involve objects and games as well as worksheets.

Kolb, therefore, imposed a structure on something that could be viewed as an informal process that takes place naturally, that of learning through experience. He suggested that it is possible to start anywhere in the cycle, but that often an action is the starting point. Kolb developed his ideas about experiential learning into theories about learning styles, reflecting the four elements of his learning cycle. You will find more information about learning styles in Chapter 4.

THEORY AND PRACTICE LINKS

Applying Kolb's cycle

Choose a lesson that you have taught recently and make this your starting point for working through Kolb's learning cycle. This will correspond to the concrete action part of the cycle. Now move through the other elements of the cycle, noting down the thoughts that come to mind at each stage (work clockwise through the cycle).

When you have worked through the cycle, use your notes as a means of evaluating the lesson. How would you do things differently in future? What would you do that was the same?

Korthagen's ALCAT model

Korthagen (1988) proposes a model for reflection, called the ALCAT model. ALCAT is an acronym for a five stage process of reflection, as follows:

- Action
- Looking back
- Creating alternative methods of action
- Awareness of essential aspects
- Trial

Korthagen and Kessels (1999) give a series of questions that can be used to move through each phase of the cycle:

QUESTIONS ASSOCIATED WITH EACH ELEMENT OF THE ALCAT CYCLE:

Action:

- What did I want to achieve or try out?

Looking back:

- What did I want/do/think/feel?

Creating alternatives:

- How can I make use of what I have discovered?
- What are the advantages and disadvantages?
- What should I do next time?

Awareness of essential aspects:

- What is the connection between the answers to the previous questions?
- What is the influence of the school as a whole and what does that mean for me?
- What is the problem or positive discovery?

Trial [same as for Action]

Their starting point is teacher education, since they express concerns that many approaches to teacher training have a narrow focus on skills and competencies that show little evidence of the integration of theory and practice, treating both as separate aspects of a teacher training curriculum. Their reflective questions, allied to the ALCAT model, are designed to assist reflection in relation to theories and models, thus addressing the issue of the integration of theory and practice.

Harri-Augstein and Thomas: self-organised learning

Self-organised learning (SOL) is an approach to managing learning that has its origins in George Kelly's Personal Construct Psychology (Kelly 1955). Harri-Augstein and Thomas's work examines learning within the framework of PCP. The PCP view of learning emphasises the learner's *constructs* about his or her learning. A construct is defined by Kelly as 'a way in which two or more things are alike and thereby different from a third', so a construct involves a process of discrimination through which we make sense of the world. These constructs are formed as a result of our experiences, which provide evidence for the discriminations that we make.

For example, if our experiences of learning as children have involved adults telling us that we find learning more difficult than others, then this is what we will come to believe and we will behave *as if* this is the case. Whenever we are in a situation that involves learning, we will make a negative prediction that we are likely to fail and behave accordingly.

SOL takes the idea of constructs related to learning and combines this with the approach of Rogers, where a client- or student-centred approach is emphasised. Therefore, SOL involves both 'teacher' and 'learner' but the notion of 'teacher' is not in a didactic role, but in keeping with a humanistic, person-centred approach; is that of a facilitator.

Harri-Augstein and Thomas define learning as 'a consciously controlled process, which allows us to improve the quality of our meanings and our actions' (Harri-Augstein and Thomas 1992). This means that learning is owned by the learner and can therefore be explored in order to increase effectiveness. It aims to give learners insight into their learning and then to use this insight in order to become more effective learners.

In order to achieve this aim the learner moves through a cyclical process of goal-setting, action, reflection (see above for a discussion about reflection) and further goal-setting arising from the outcomes of the learner's reflections. The process of moving through this cycle is via what Thomas and Harri-Augstein call a *learning conversation*. They call their self-organised learning approach a *conversational* one:

> Self-organisation consists in the ability to converse with oneself about one's own learning processes and to observe, search, analyse, formulate, judge, decide and act on the basis of such creative encounters. This involves as much feeling as thought. Unaided, most people are not able to generate effective learning conversations with themselves or with others.

Table 10.1 shows the stages of a learning conversation with an example of each stage.

A learning conversation can be carried out without anyone else present. However, Harri-Augstein and Thomas introduce the notion of a 'learning coach'. This is an individual who guides and supports the learner through the learning conversation. The coach would use open-ended questions to assist the learner to move

Table 10.1   Stages of a learning conversation

Stage	Explanation and example
Topic	Planning my teaching
Task (related to the topic)	Complete my long-term planning sheets
Purposes	A target to be achieved. A purpose might be derived by looking at previous attempts. In this example, the purpose might be: ● to complete my planning sheets during my non-contact time so I don't have to take them home at the weekend. Note that the description is quite observable. This is to facilitate subsequent stages when you might note specific observations that form the evidence for deciding whether you have achieved your purpose.
Strategy	The strategy is what you will actually do in order to achieve your purpose. As with the purpose, observable descriptions are helpful and an influence might be the learner's past history (previous attempts). The learner can identify more than one strategy. In the example, the learner's strategies might be: ● I will work where I won't be disturbed; ● I will only take this work with me so I don't end up doing another task instead.
Outcome	This is a description of the criteria for success: How will I know I've achieved my purpose? The outcome might involve the learner in making some statement about his or her feelings, as well as giving some measurable criteria by which to judge success in achieving purposes. In this example, the outcome might be: ● I will finish the planning sheets and be able to hand them in to the head before I go home; ● I will not take this work home; ● I will feel more relaxed at the weekend and will have time to go to the pub.
Review	This stage involves thinking about what the learner actually did. In order to carry out this stage, the learner might go through a sub-stage between outcome and review, which involves making a record of what actually happened. The first part of the review is to use the record of action in order to think about any differences between what was planned and what actually happened: a process of considering 'before' and 'after' behaviour.

(*continued*)

Table 10.1 Continued

Stage	Explanation and example
	This process then leads to a consideration of strengths and weaknesses.
	The information is then used to plan a new set of purposes, and the cycle begins again.
	In the example given, the learner might review as follows:
	• I didn't finish the sheets so I had to take them home;
	• I did find somewhere quiet to work;
	• I was side-tracked because the secretary asked me to take a phone call;
	• my strength was that I did find a quiet place to wok and was focused on the one task I wanted to finish;
	• my weakness was that I allowed myself to be interrupted;
	• I felt cross because I really wanted to hand the sheets in so I could forget about school for at least part of the weekend. I felt more stressed at the weekend;
	• next time I will put a 'do not disturb' sign on the door and ask the secretary to take a message if I have any phone calls.

through the cycle of purpose, strategy, outcome and review. Harri-Augstein and Thomas comment:

> The S-O-L coach temporarily externalises this 'Learning Conversation' to improve its quality. . . . S/he makes the nature of the conversation explicit to the learner so that he or she can appreciate its nature and what it can achieve, gradually passing control of the learning conversation to the learner as awareness and skill develops. (ibid. 1992)

As Harri-Augstein and Thomas commented earlier, a learning conversation can be held with oneself. However, if this is the method used, then the process will be assisted by a number of prompts in order to aid reflection and movement through the cycle of purpose, strategy, outcome and review. The following contains an application activity that should help you to conduct a learning conversation and includes the type of prompts that a learning coach might use to help you.

THEORY AND PRACTICE LINKS

Carrying out a learning conversation

Select a topic area and task, then carry out your learning conversation by filling in the grid below (Table 10.2).

Table 10.2   Practical example: carrying out a learning conversation

Stage of learning conversation	Questions	My notes
Purpose	What are my purposes? How did I do this in the past and what did I learn as a result? How can this information shape my purposes?	
Strategies	What actions am I going to take in order to achieve my purpose(s)? What strategies have I used in the past and how successful were they?	
Outcome	How will I know I have achieved my purpose? How will I feel?	
Review step 1: Record of action	What did I actually do?	
Review step 2: Differences	What did I plan/predict and what actually happened? Using the record of action, what differences were there in my purposes, strategies and outcomes?	
Review step 3: Strengths and weaknesses	Thinking about the differences, what are my strengths and weaknesses?	
Review step 4: New/revised purposes	What should my new purposes be?	

Summary: the reflective teacher

This part of the chapter has attempted to 'unpick' the idea of what is meant by reflection and the reflective teacher. We have given you some tools to use so that you can engage in the process of reflection. The goal of engaging in this process should be to enhance your teaching. If you are an effective and insightful learner, we would suggest that this, in turn, will have a positive impact on your pupils. Some of the strategies that have been introduced, notably self-organised learning, can be used with children and young people; this approach is not just for adult learners. As a further application, therefore, you might also wish to consider carrying out learning conversations with your pupils as well as with yourself.

Learning from evidence: teachers and research

The term 'evidence-based practice', or learning from evidence, is becoming more common in educational circles. It was originally used in relation to the practice of medicine (see, for example, Sackett *et al.* 1996) and in this context was defined broadly as the way in which research evidence is combined with practitioners' clinical judgements and patients' needs or views. Such an approach has been promoted by the Department of Health.

This section will examine what is meant by the term 'evidence'. It will then go on to look at some common aspects of educational research that will help you to make sense of research reports and papers.

What is 'evidence'?

'Evidence' is one of those words that is used so widely that we rarely stop to consider what it actually means. The word is loaded with assumptions we might have about what knowledge is and how we think we can make sense of the world around us.

When we think about the word 'evidence' we might have in mind some kind of objective scientific process. We assume that there is an objective reality that can be studied scientifically. This kind of approach would involve collecting some data and then deducing a cause-and-effect relationship after we have looked at the data. An example might help here: Suppose you went to a training course about a new way to teach children to read. The authors of the method tell the audience of teachers that they have evidence that this new method is very effective. They show you the results of an experiment they carried out. They used the new method with one group of children and not with another. The group that received the new method made more progress in reading. The authors conclude that this new method should therefore be used with all children.

What are the assumptions being made here? We would suggest that:

- the idea that an experiment can be conducted with people assumes that they can be viewed as being in a laboratory, where conditions are controlled;

- as consequence of the first assumption, the two groups are assumed to have identical experiences, with the exception of the method of teaching reading;

- there is an assumption that nothing else that could account for the results; and,

- therefore, a cause-and-effect relationship is assumed between the new method of teaching and the increased progress made by the children involved in the experiment.

If we accept these assumptions, we might leave the course and go back to school full of enthusiasm that, at last, we have found a way to teach reading that has been *proved* to be effective.

Perhaps, however, we might stop to think and look a little more closely at the claims that are made. What would your view be if you found out that the experiment was carried out in a university using the lecturers' children, or that the new method was only used for two weeks, or that the group that did not receive the new method were not taught reading at all? You might think twice before spending the year's literacy budget on this method. The reasons for the doubts creeping in are related to the assumptions on which the claims are based. Given your experience of children, young people and schools, can we really assume that we can study them objectively? If we think we can, then we are assuming that all individuals are the same.

We would suggest that it is very difficult to study children, young people and schools in a completely objective manner. The idea that there is an 'objective reality' is a very entrenched western philosophical idea. This type of world view was called 'positivist' by the philosopher Auguste Comte in 1844. He suggested that human thinking went through stages of development, the final stage of which was positivist, where objectivity and reason were paramount. Allied to this notion of positivism was the scientific approach that was alluded to earlier, where objectivity and cause-and-effect are viewed as the important constituents of knowledge. Additionally, the notion of *empiricism* is part of the positivist view; that is, that experience is the only source of true knowledge. Therefore, knowledge is acquired through a process of *inductive reasoning*, that is, where information is gathered and then is analysed in order to derive rules and principles (the opposing view being that knowledge is based on intuition).

The reason for the philosophical discussion in the preceding paragraph is that it is an important step in considering what is meant by 'evidence'. One such view, as discussed in the previous paragraph, is that we define evidence in terms of objectivity and cause-and-effect relationships. In addition, when we come to look specifically at research, you will see that some models of research are based on this positivist viewpoint.

We have suggested that one of the problems with a positivist view is that 'life isn't like that'. This brings us to the opposite view. If we do not accept that we can view knowledge as objective, then the opposite is that we experience the world subjectively. This brings us back to the notion of existentialism, discussed at the beginning of this chapter, which in turn is reflected in humanistic psychology. This subjective view is sometimes called an *anti-positivist* view. This view states that we cannot be completely objective about the social world, since society and the people in it do not behave in a predictable way. Therefore, we can only understand human behaviour by being involved, as it is not possible to be an objective outsider. Campbell *et al.* (2004) express this view in their comment: 'ringing true rather than being true'.

The heading to this section posed the question 'What is evidence?'. We have seen that, in terms of working with children and young people within complex and differing school systems, it is not possible to give a neat definition that relates to the objective collection and analysis of information. Nisbet's comment is illuminating: 'Thus "answers" to problems depend on how we conceptualise the problem, and this in turn is often dependent on the metaphors we use to grapple with and analyse the issues' (Nisbet 2005).

Evidence, therefore, is not simply facts and figures; it can also be seen as the way in which a set of findings about a particular issue in education might have meaning for individuals involved in similar circumstances or contexts. In this scenario, Campbell *et al.*'s notion of 'ringing true' would be a valid definition of evidence.

The two views of knowledge discussed above – that of the positivist and anti-positivist views – are the bases for approaches to research. The following sections will describe these different approaches.

The positivist view: experimental and quasi-experimental research

Research arising from a positivist tradition takes a scientific approach to what is being studied. This is done by applying specific controls in order to derive a cause-and-effect relationship from the results obtained. The use of the label 'experimental' means that whatever is being studied is done so as if it were a laboratory experiment. Therefore, variables (that is, things that are subject to change) are identified and then manipulated so that the effects of any changes can be observed.

True experimental research uses *randomised controlled trials*. This means that the researcher compares two groups. The composition of each group is done in a random fashion in order to ensure that variables are controlled and that each group is a representative sample of the population as a whole; so, effectively, it can be assumed that both groups are the same.

The example we gave earlier about the new method of teaching reading may be used to show the way in which experimental research is carried out. The authors claimed that their new method of teaching reading was effective. To use terminology associated with experimental research, their *hypothesis* is that method A of teaching reading will lead to increased progress in reading. In this experiment, there are two types of variable: the *independent variable*; that is, the variable which is changed (in this case the method of teaching reading) and the *dependent variable*, that is, the one which is measured or observed (in this case progress in reading). After identifying the hypothesis and the independent and dependent variables, the researchers would follow this procedure:

● Identify a group of children in a particular year group (in order to control the variable of the effects of age and development, it would not be appropriate to have a range of ages).

- Randomly assign children to a control or experimental group.

- Collect some data before the experiment begins. In this case, the researchers would test the children's reading.

- Make a change to the independent variable for the experimental group. The change here would be to use the new method of teaching reading. The control group would not have any changes made to the independent variable.

- At the end of a set period of time, the same tests or measurements that were carried out before the experiment are carried out again.

- The results for each group are compared. If the experimental group have made more progress in reading than the control group, the researchers will attribute the increased progress to the change that they made; that is, the new way of teaching reading.

Sometimes it is not possible to carry out random assignment to groups. For example, in a school it might be difficult to do so because it might go against other organising principles such as age or ability. Where random assignment is not possible, a control and experimental group is still used but the groups are not random. For example, in our experiment, described above, a quasi-experimental approach would mean that, for example, the control and experimental groups comprised two Year 5 classes in the school.

When experimental research is carried out, issues about *reliability* and *validity* have to be addressed. If an experiment is *reliable*, it should do what it sets out to do consistently. For example, if our experiment involved observing something and then rating it, we have to be assured that we would both give very similar ratings. If our experiment is *valid*, we are saying that it measures what it is supposed to measure. So, in our example of looking at a new way of teaching reading, our findings might not be considered valid if we tested children's language and assumed that this told us something about their reading. In experimental research, the terms internal and external validity are used. Internal validity asks whether the intervention made a difference to the subjects and external validity asks whether the findings can be generalised. There is a range of factors to consider in relation to validity (called threats to validity); it is outside the scope of this book to go into detail about these, but the reader is directed to Cohen and Manion (1989) for further, very clear information about this aspect of experimental and quasi-experimental research. Their comments about validity are helpful in explaining the concept:

> By way of summary, we have seen that an experiment can be said to be internally valid to the extent that within its own confines its results are credible, but for those results to be useful they must be generalisable beyond the confines of the particular experiment: in a word, they must be externally valid also.

Experimental and quasi-experimental research

Mr Ivor E. Tower is a teacher with great enthusiasm for 'projects'. He is interested in finding out all sorts of things about practice in education. He has lots of good ideas but needs some help in pinning down exactly what it is he should be looking at. Some of his ideas are given below. Read each one and them; then:

- State the hypothesis.
- Identify the independent variable.
- Identify the dependent variable.
- Suggest how you might collect data about the dependent variable.

Bright idea 1

Children these days don't eat properly. I think that giving them breakfast at school will make them concentrate better.

Bright idea 2

We don't have time to develop all the skills and abilities of our pupils through extra-curricular activities. If we did chess, our pupils would be so much better at maths.

Bright idea 3

I don't believe that children should be given cubes or counters when they're learning maths; it just makes them lazy. They would learn much better without all this 'apparatus'.

Bright idea 4

Children don't listen to stories any more. If they did they would be much better readers.

These examples raise issues related to ethics in research, which we haven't considered in detail. Think about these points:

- What right do we have to 'experiment' on children? What about consent?

In the scenario illustrated in Bright idea 1, there is a potential ethical issue related to having a control and experimental group. What is this?

Anti-positivist research: contextualised or naturalistic research

The anti-positivist tradition views knowledge as subjective and therefore asserts that we cannot treat the world as a laboratory in which we can carry out controlled experiments. The research that arises from this view accepts that humans have different values and experiences and does not, therefore, try to control variables in the same way that experimental research does. Campbell *et al.* (2004) call this type of research *naturalistic* research, commenting:

So this research tradition emphasises the context-specific nature of all stages of its methodology, from the initial formulation of a particular problem through to whatever tentative and highly provisional conclusions might be produced which are also, of course, context-specific.

Action Research is a term used to describe contextualised or naturalistic research. This is defined by Carr and Kemmis (1986) as 'self-reflective enquiry'. This approach, therefore, takes us right back to the beginning of this chapter where we examined the notions of reflection and the reflective practitioner. Cohen and Manion (1989) identify characteristics of action research, as follows:

- it is contextual;
- data are collected over time;
- a range of data-collection methods are used (for example, diaries, case studies or questionnaires); and
- feedback is designed to effect change to the context being studied; it is applied immediately.

There are three basic phases in action research:

- look: where information is gathered, the context for the research is described and a definition of what is being researched is developed;
- think: where the data are interpreted and reflected on; and
- act: where solutions are formulated and acted upon.

Cohen and Manion expand on these three basic stages by suggesting eight stages, as follows:

- formulate the problem;
- formulate a proposal by negotiating with stakeholders (that is, those individuals with an interest in the problem);
- look at the literature to find out how others have tackled the problem;
- in the light of any information from literature, modify or refine the problem or proposal;
- decide what type of data collection or procedure will be used;
- choose evaluation procedures;
- implement the research/project; and
- interpret and evaluate.

In order to illustrate the process, we will take the basic example that we used in the previous section (a new method of teaching reading) and show how an action research process might deal with a reading problem in a school.

An example of action research

The head teacher of a school had just completed her 'round' of classroom observations of staff. One thing she felt unhappy about was the way in which they were teaching reading. Rather than impose this view on the staff (and she did not want to assume that all staff shared this view), she raised the issue at a staff meeting in order to find out what other staff thought.

At the staff meeting, she found that other staff shared her view that they could make changes for the better. At subsequent staff meetings, they talked further about how they were teaching reading in order to be more focused on what they thought the specific problems were. After a process of negotiation and discussion, they decided that they needed to look at reading comprehension. The head and the literacy co-ordinator did some further investigation of this aspect of reading and as a result suggested a specific way of teaching that they felt would be helpful. This was discussed with the staff and all agreed that they thought it was worth trying out. They decided that they would implement this method at the beginning of the next term, run it for a term and then evaluate progress. Parents were kept informed via the school newsletter and at parents' evening, where a display board was set up.

They decided that they wanted a number of different perspectives about this new method, so as well as using information from the reading screening tests used routinely in school, they decided to note down their thoughts about the method as part of their planning and evaluation. They also decided to carry out some additional assessment of children's reading comprehension, as this was the focus of the new method. It was important for them to have information about the practicalities of implementing this new method because they were aware that there are many demands on teacher time. They also decided to ask the pupils and parents what they thought, so two questionnaires were drawn up.

The staff implemented this new method for a term and at the end of this period they used one of their training days to look at all the information that had been collected. Using the data, they decided that the new method had made a difference so they agreed that they would continue to use it.

Some points to consider:

- One aspect of research is about generalisability. It could be argued that whatever the findings of this research, they could not be generalised to another school. Does this matter?

- In this research, the enquiry arose from a genuine need within the school.

- The research was collaborative; it involved all staff in helping to formulate the research question and investigate it.

- Parents and pupils were involved as well. Does this reduce concerns about the ethics of research, in relation to consent?

Analysing data from research

When a research project has been carried out, there will be a large amount of data or information. These have to be analysed in order to find some answers to the questions being examined. This section will give a brief overview of some of the ways in which data from research can be analysed.

Data are often grouped into two main categories: quantitative and qualitative. *Quantitative* data are concerned with numbers and are usually obtained from some kind of tests or measurements that produce scores (in the example of our teaching reading experiment, the results were in the form of scores from reading tests). *Qualitative* data, in contrast, do not use numbers or scores. These data might be things like the content of a reflective diary (for example, in our action research example, teachers were asked to keep a note of their thoughts about the new teaching method), transcripts of conversations or classroom interactions.

One aspect of data analysis that you might come across if you read research reports is the use of statistics. Sometimes numerical data are analysed using statistical tests. The purpose of this is to determine the level of significance, that is, the likelihood that the results could have been obtained by chance. Significance is expressed as p. The value of p, obtained by subjecting the data to statistical analysis, tells the researcher and his/her audience how far we can attribute the results obtained to the intervention (if you remember, cause-and-effect relationships are part of a positivist approach). Therefore, if the statistical test gives a value for p that is thought to be significant, the researchers are able to say with some confidence that their results were not just obtained by chance (that is, the changes would have happened anyway, without the intervention). In experimental and quasi-experimental research, the accepted value for p is less than 0.01. This means that there is only a 1 per cent (or 1 in 100) probability that the results happened by chance. Basically, the higher the level of p, the less reliable the results are thought to be.

Some research data are used to look at *correlations*. A correlation looks at relationships between sets of data. Statistical tests giving correlation coefficients can be used to indicate the strength of the relationship. However, a correlation is not the same as a cause-and-effect relationship. A correlation between two sets of data tells us that there is some relationship. For example, there might be a correlation between academic achievement and socio-economic status of the family. This does not mean that one causes the other, simply that there is a relationship.

Clearly, statistics can only be used to analyse quantitative data. The analysis of qualitative data can be complex and time-consuming. Consider our action research example. If there are 200 pupils in the school, then up to 400 questionnaires will have to be analysed. The evaluative comments of up to ten teachers will have to be analysed. Qualitative data are not examined in order to 'prove' or support a cause-and-effect relationship; they are examined to help the researcher make sense of the situation that s/he is working in or alongside. Trends and patterns might be an outcome of an analysis, but not causality. Robson (1993) suggests some general strategies for analysis that relate to using the original theory or proposition that gave rise to the research or creating a framework for analysing in order to generate some principles.

In summary, there are a number of ways of analysing research data. The type of analysis depends on the approach taken and the type of data collected (numerical or non-numerical). It has only been possible to give a very brief outline in this section. Readers are directed to either Cohen and Manion (1989) or Robson (1993) for detailed information about data analysis.

Summary

This chapter has covered two aspects of teachers' professional development: becoming a reflective practitioner; and the process of research. We would like to finish by suggesting that these two topics are, and should be, closely related. A reflective practitioner is undergoing a systematic process of thought and evaluation in order to improve practice. In the same way, research is a systematic process that, in an anti-positivist approach, can involve reflection and action in relation to one's own context. This is the very essence of practitioner research, which should be valued just as much as what we might view as the traditional, experimental approach. Systematic reflection and action should lead to appropriate and contextual change that has a direct impact on the pupils that you teach. We therefore encourage you to follow up the content of this chapter by reading research and reflecting on its value to you as a practitioner.

References

Adey, P., Shayer, M. and Yates, C. (1995) *Thinking Science*. London: Thomas Nelson and Sons.

Arnold, C. (2002) 'The dynamics of reading acquisition – applications of chaos theory to literacy development'. Unpublished PhD thesis. University of Wolverhampton.

Arnold, C. and Yeomans, J. (2005) *Psychology for Teaching Assistants*. Stoke-on-Trent: Trentham Press.

Arnold, D. (1967) 'More Monteverdi vespers'. *Musical Times*, 108, 637–8.

Asperger, H. (1944) Die autistichen psychopathen im kindersaller. *Archiv fur Psychiatrie und Nervenkrankenheiten*; 117, 76–136.

Asperger, H. (1979) 'Problems of infantile autism'. *Communication*, 13, 45–52.

Assessment Reform Group (1999) *Assessment for Learning: Beyond the Black Box*. Cambridge: University of Cambridge Faculty of Education.

Atkinson, R. and Shiffrin, R. (1968) 'Human memory: a proposed system and its control processes', in K. Spence and J. Spence (eds) *The Psychology of Learning and Motivation: Advances in Research and Theory* (Volume 2). New York: Academic Press.

Augustinos, M. and Rosewarne, D.L. (2001) 'Stereotype knowledge and prejudice in children'. *British Journal of Developmental Psychology*, 19, 143–56.

Ausabel, D. (1963) *The Psychology of Meaningful Verbal Learning*. New York: Grune and Stratton.

Ausabel, D. (1968) *Educational Psychology: A Cognitive View*. London: Holt, Reinhart & Winston.

Barrow, G., Bradshaw, E. and Newton, T. (2001) *Improving Behaviour and Raising Self-Esteem in the Classroom: A Practical Guide to Using Transactional Analysis*. London: David Fulton Publishers.

Bavelas (1965) cited in Rosenthal, R. and Jacobson, L. (1992) as personal comm. (ch. 1:6).

Benton, P. and O'Brien, T. (2000) *Special Needs and the Beginning Teacher*. London: Continuum.

Best, C. and Avery, R. (1999) 'Left-hemisphere advantage for click consonants is determined by linguistic significance and experience'. *Psychological Science*, 10, 65–70.

Bettelheim, B. (1967) *The Empty Fortress: Infantile Autism and the Birth of the Self*. New York: Free Press.

Binet, A. and Simon, T. (1916) *The Development of Intelligence in Children*. Baltimore, MD: Williams and Wilkins.

Black, P., Harrison, C., Lee, C., Marshall, B. and Wiliam, D. (2002) *Working Inside the Black Box: Assessment for Learning in the Classroom*. London: King's College.

Bollmer, J.M., Milich, R., Harris, M.J. and Maras, M.A. (2005) 'A friend in need: the role of friendship quality as a protective factor in peer victimization and bullying'. *Journal of Interpersonal Violence*, 20(6), 701–12.

Bowlby, J. (1951) *Maternal Care and Mental Health*. Geneva: WHO.

Boxall, M. (2003) *Nurture Groups in Schools: Principles and Practice*. London: Paul Chapman.

Broadbent, D. (1958) *Perception and Communication*. London: Pergamon Press.

Bruner, J. (1960) *The Process of Education*. Cambridge, MA: Harvard University Press.

Burt, C. (1927) *The Young Delinquent*. London: University of London Press.

Buss, D.M., Larsen, R.J., Westen, D. and Semmelroth, J. (1992) 'Sex differences in jealousy: evolution, physiology, and psychology'. *Psychological Science*, **33**, 251–5.

Calderwood, P. (2000) *Learning Community: Finding Common Ground in Difference*. New York: Teachers College, Columbia University.

Camodeca, M. and Goossens, F. (2005) 'Children's opinions on effective strategies to cope with bullying: the importance of bullying role and perspective'. *Educational Research*, **47**(1), 93–105, March.

Campbell, A., McNamara, O. and Gilroy, P. (2004) *Practitioner Research and Professional Development in Education*. London: Paul Chapman Publishing.

Canter, L. and Canter, M. (1992) *Lee Canter's Assertive Discipline: Positive Behaviour Management for Today's Classroom*. Santa Monica, CA: Canter and Associates.

Carr, W. and Kemmis, S. (1986) *Becoming Critical. Education, Knowledge and Action Research*. Lewes: Falmer.

Carraher, T.N., Carraher, D. and Schliemann, A.D. (1985) 'Mathematics on the streets and in schools'. *British Journal of Developmental Psychology*, **3**, 21–9.

Cattell, R.B. (1963) 'Theory of fluid and crystallised intelligence: a critical experiment'. *Journal of Educational Psychology*, **54**, 1–22.

Central Advisory Council for Education (1967) *Children and Their Primary Schools* (The Plowden Report). London: HMSO.

Chitiyo, M. and Wheeler, J. (2004) 'The development of special educational services in Zimbabwe'. *International Journal of Special Education*, **19**(2), 46–52.

Coffield, F., Moseley, D., Hall, E. and Ecclestone, K. (2004) *Should We Be Using Learning Styles? What Research Has to Say to Practice*. London: Learning and Skills Research Centre.

Cohen, L. and Manion, L. (1989) *Research Methods in Education* (3rd edn). London: Routledge.

Cox and Klinger (1988) 'A motivational model of alcohol use'. *Journal of Abnormal Child Psychology*, **97**(2), 168–80, May.

Crowley, C., Hallam, S., Harre, R. and Lunt, I. (2001) 'Study support for young people with same-sex attraction – views and experiences from a pioneering peer support initiative in the north of England'. *Educational and Child Psychology*, **18**(1), 89–107.

Day, C. (1999) *Developing Teachers: The Challenge of Lifelong Learning*. London: Falmer Press.

Department of Education and Science (1981) *The School Curriculum*. London: DES.

Department of Education and Science (1989) *Discipline in Schools* (The Elton Report). London: HMSO.

Department for Education and Skills (2002) *Bullying: Don't Suffer in Silence: An Anti-Bullying Pack for Schools*. Nottingham: DfES.

Department for Education and Skills (2003) *Every Child Matters*. London: The Stationery Office.

Department for Education and Skills (2004) *Assessment for Learning in Everyday Lessons*. London: DfES.

Department for Education and Skills (2005) *Excellence and Enjoyment: Social and Emotional Aspects of Learning*. London: DfES.

Deutsch, J. and Deutsch, D. (1963) 'Attention: some theoretical considerations'. *Psychological Review*, **70**, 80–90.

Dewey, J. (1916) *Democracy and Education: An Introduction to the Philosophy of Education*. New York: Free Press.

Dewey, J. (1938) *Experience and Education*. New York: Kappa Delta Pi.

Division of Educational and Child Psychology (1999) *Dyslexia, Literacy and Psychological Assessment*. Leicester: British Psychological Society.

Donaldson, M. (1978) *Children's Minds*. Glasgow: William Collins/Fontana.

Dovidio, J. and Gaertner, S. (1986) *Prejudice, Discrimination and Racism*. London: Academic Press.

Dunbar, R. (1993) 'Coevolution of neocortex as a constraint on group processes'. *Behavioural Brain Science*, **16**, 681–735.

Dunbar, R. (2003) 'The social brain: mind, language and society in evolutionary perspective'. *Annual Review of Anthropology*, **32**, 163–81.

Eberhardt, J.L. and Fiske S.T. (eds) (1998) *Confronting Racism: The Problem and the Response*. Thousand Oaks CA: Sage Publications Inc., pp. 137–63.

Elinoff, M.J., Chafouleas, S.M. and Sassu, K.A. (2004) 'Bullying: considerations for defining and intervening in school settings'. *Psychology in the Schools*, **41**(8), 887–97.

Elliot, C.D. (1997) *The British Ability Scales*. Windsor: National Foundation for Educational Research.

Elliott, J. (2000) 'Dynamic assessment in educational contexts: purpose and promise', in C. Lidz and J. Elliott (eds) *Dynamic Assessment: Prevailing Models and Applications*. New York: Elsevier.

Ellis, R. (1985) *Understanding Second Language Acquisition*. Oxford: Oxford University Press.

Entwistle, N. and Kozeki, B. (1985) 'Relationships between school motivation, approaches to studying and attainment among British and Hungarian adolescents'. *British Journal of Educational Psychology*, **55**(2), 124–37.

Erikson, E.H. (1950) *Childhood and Society*. New York: Norton.

Eysenck, H. (1987) 'Speed of information processing, reaction time and the theory of intelligence', in P.A. Vernon (ed.) *Speed of Information Processing and Intelligence*. Norwood, NJ: Ablex.

Feurstein, R., Feurstein, R.S., Falik, L.H. and Rand, Y. (2002) *The Dynamic Assessment of Cognitive Modifiability*. Jerusalem: ICELP Press.

Freeman (1991) In *Educating the Very Able* (2003). London: OFSTED.

Freeman (1997) In *Educating the Very Able* (2003). London: OFSTED.

Freud, S. (1905) Three essays on the theory of sexuality, in Standard Edition, Vol. 7, pp. 130–243.

Friedman, M. and Rosenman R.H. (1974), cited in Stevens, R. (ed.) (1996) *Understanding the Self*. London: Sage.

Frost, L.A. and Bondy, A.S. (1994) *The Picture Exchange Communication System: Training Manual*. Cherry Hill, NJ: Pyramid Educational Consultants Inc.

Furnham, A. (2000) 'Thinking about intelligence'. *The Psychologist*, **13**(10), 510–15.

Galton, F. (1883) *Inquiries into Human Faculty and its Development*. London: Macmillan.

Gardner, H. (1983) *Frames of Mind: The Theory of Multiple Intelligence*. New York: Basic Books.

Gardner, H. and Hatch, T. (1989) 'Multiple intelligences go to school: educational implications of the theory of multiple intelligence'. *Educational Researcher*, **18**, 4–9.

Garrett, H. (1966) *Statistics in Psychology and Education*. New York: David McKay Company.

Geertz, C. (1968) 'Religion as cultural system', in D.Cutler (ed.) *The Religious Situation*. Boston, MA: Beacon Press.

Ginwright, S.A. (2004) *Black in School – Afrocentric Reform, Urban Youth, and the Promise of Hip-hop Culture*. New York and London: Teachers College Press.

Glaser, R. (1962) *Training, Research and Education*. Pittsburgh: Pittsburgh University Press.

Glover, D., Gough, G., Johnson, M. and Cartwright, N. (2000) 'Bullying in 25 secondary schools: incidence, impact and intervention'. *Educational Research*, **42**(2), 141–56.

Goleman, D. (1995) *Emotional Intelligence*. New York: Bantam Books.

Goswami, U. (2004) 'Neuroscience and education'. *British Journal of Educational Psychology*, **74**, 1–14.

Greenhalgh, P. (1994) *Emotional Growth and Learning*. London: Routledge.

Gross, M.U.M. (1993) *Exceptionally Gifted Children*. London: Routledge.

Guilford, J.P. (1967) *The Nature of Human Intelligence*. New York: McGraw Hill.

Hall, J. (2005) *Neuroscience and Education. A Review of the Contribution of Brain Science to Teaching and Learning.* Glasgow: The Scottish Council for Research in Education.

Haring, N.G., Lovitt, T.C., Eaton, M.D. and Hansen, C.L. (1978) *The Fourth R: Research in the Classroom.* Columbus, OH: Charles E. Merrill Publishing Co.

Harri-Augstein, S. and Thomas, L. (1992) 'Self-organised learning for personal and organisation growth'. *Training and Development.* March, 26–30.

Harrop, A. and Swinson, J. (2000) 'Natural rates of approval and disapproval in British infant, junior and secondary schools'. *British Journal of Educational Psychology*, 70(4).

Hathiwala-Ward, H. and Swinson, J. (1999) 'Teachers' verbal responses in a mulit-racial primary school'. *Educational and Child Psychology*, 16(3), 37–43.

Hellaby, L. (2004) 'Teaching TA in the primary school', in G. Barrow and T. Newton (eds) *Walking the Talk: How Transactional Analysis is Improving Behaviour and Raising Self-esteem.* London: David Fulton Publishers.

Herrnstein, R. and Murray, C. (1994) *The Bell Curve: Intelligence and Class Structure in American Life.* New York: The Free Press.

Hortaçsu, N (1995) 'Parents' education levels, parents' beliefs and child outcomes'. *Journal of Genetic Psychology*, 156(3), 373–83.

Howe, K. (1995) 'Validity, bias and justice in educational testing: the limits of the consequentialist conception' (www.ed.uiuc.edu/EPS/PES-Yearbook/95_docs/howe.html – downloaded 17/05/05).

Howe, M. (1990) 'Does intelligence exist?' *The Psychologist*, November, 490–7.

Jackson, D.A. and King, A.R. (2004) 'Gender differences in the effects of oppositional behavior on teacher ratings of ADHD symptoms'. *Journal of Abnormal Child Psychology*, 32(2), 215–24.

James, W. (1905) *Text Book of Psychology*. London: Macmillan.

Jerram, H., Glynn, T. and Tuck, B. (1988) 'Responding to the message: providing a social context for children learning to write'. *Educational Psychology*, 8, 31–40.

Jones, E.E., Riggs, J.M. and Quattrone, G. (1979) 'Observer bias in the attitude attribution paradigm: effect of time and information order'. *Journal of Personality and Social Psychology*.

Kanner, L. (1943) 'Autistic disturbances of affective contact'. *Nervous Child*, 2, 217–50.

Kelly, G. (1955) *The Psychology of Personal Constructs*. New York: Norton.

Killen, M., McLaughlin, N., Margie, N. and Sinno, S. (2005) 'Minority children's intergroup attitudes about peer group relationships'. *British Journal of Developmental Psychology*, 23(2), 251–69.

Kilworth, M., Bernard, H.R. and McCarty, C. (1984) 'Measuring patterns of acquaintanship'. *Current Anthropology*, 25, 391–7.

Knowles, M. (1984) *The Adult Learner: A Neglected Species* (3rd edn). Houston, TX: Gulf Publishing.

Kohn, A. (1999) *Punished by Rewards*. Boston, MA: Houghton Mifflin.

Kolb, D. (1984) *Experiential Learning: Experience as the Source of Learning and Development*. Englewood Cliffs, NJ: Prentice-Hall Inc.

Koren, I., Kolesaric, V. and Dragutin, I. (1992) 'Analysis of the causes of school underachievement among intellectually superior students'. *Sovremena Psihologija*, 1(1–2), 7–30.

Korthagen, F. (1988) 'The influence of learning orientations on the development of reflective teaching', in M. Fuller and A. Rosie (eds). *Teacher Education and School Partnerships*. New York: Edwin Mellen Press.

Korthagen, F. and Kessels, J. (1999) 'Linking theory and practice: changing the pedagogy of teacher education'. *Educational Researcher*, 28(4), 4–17.

Kuit, J., Reay, G. and Freemans, R. (2001) 'Experiences of reflective teaching. *Active Learning in Higher Education*, 2(2), 128–142.

Lam, S., Pui-shan, Y., Law, J.S.F. and Cheung, R.W.Y. (2004) 'The effects of competition on achievement motivation in Chinese classrooms'. *British Journal of Educational Psychology*, **74**, 281–96.

Langer, E.J. and Rodin, J. (1976) 'The effects of choice and enhanced personal responsibility for the aged'. *Journal of Personality and Social Psychology*, **34**(2), 191–8, August.

Lawrence, R. (1991) 'The integrity of culture'. *American Behavioural Scientist*, **34**(5), 594–617.

Littleford, L.N., Wright, M.O. and Sayoc-Parial, M. (2005) 'White students' intergroup anxiety during same-race and interracial interactions: a multimethod approach'. *Basic and Applied Social Psychology*, **27**(1), 85–94, March.

Lohr, B., Adams, H., and Davis, M. (1997) 'Sexual arousal to erotic and aggressive stimuli in sexually coercive and noncoercive men'. *Journal of Abnormal Psychology*, **106**(2), 230–42.

Lucas, P. (1991) 'Reflection, new practices and the need for flexibility in supervising student teachers'. *Journal of Further and Higher Education*, **15**(2), 84–93.

McGlothlin, H., Killen, M. and Edmonds, C. (2005) 'European-American children's intergroup attitudes about peer relationships'. *British Journal of Developmental Psychology*, **23**, 227–49.

McGuiness, C. (1999) *From Thinking Skills to Thinking Classrooms: A Review and Evaluation of Approaches for Developing Pupils' Thinking*. London: DfEE Research Report RR115.

McNaughton, S., Glynn, T. and Robinson, V. (1987) *Pause, Prompt and Praise: Effective Tutoring for Remedial Reading*. Birmingham: Positive Products.

McPherson, W. (1999) *The Stephen Lawrence Enquiry*. London: The Stationery Office.

Mager, R. (1975) *Preparing Instructional Objectives* (2nd edn). Belmont, CA: Lake Publishing Co.

Merriman, H. and Arnold, C. (2006) *Perceptions of Extended School Activities*. Presentation to DECP conference, January. Leicester: British Psychological Society.

Midwinter, E. (1972). *Priority Education: An Account of the Liverpool Project*. Harmondsworth: Penguin.

Miller, A. (2003) *Teachers, Parents and Classroom Behaviour: A Psychosocial Approach*. Maidenhead: OU Press/McGraw-Hill Education.

Miller, G.A. (1956) 'The magical number seven, plus or minus two: some limits on our capacity for processing information'. *Psychological Review*, **63**, 81–97.

Morris, D. (1990) *Animal Watching*. London: Cape.

Neill, A.S. (1992) *The New Summerhill* (ed. A. Lamb). Harmondsworth: Penguin.

Nelson, J., Lott, L. and Glenn, H. (2000) *Positive Discipline in the Classroom*. New York: Three Rivers Press.

Newson, E. and Newson, J. (1963) *Patterns of Infant Care in an Urban Community*. Harmondsworth, Penguin.

Nguy, L. and Hunt, C.J. (2004) 'Ethnicity and bullying: a study of Australian high-school students'. *Educational and Child Psychology*, **21**(4), 78–94.

Nisbet, J. (2005) 'What is educational research? Changing perspectives through the 20th century'. *Research Papers in Education*, **20**(1), 25–44.

Nisbett, R.E., Caputo, C., Legant, P. and Maracek, J. (1973) 'Behavior as seen by the actor and as seen by the observer'. *Journal of Personality and Social Psychology*, **27**, 154–64.

Olweus, D. (1993) *Bullying at School*. London: Blackwell.

Paivio, A. (1986) *Mental Representations*. New York: Oxford University Press.

Pawson, R. and Tilley, N. (1997) *Realistic Evaluation*. London: Sage.

Petrides, K., Chamorro-Premuzic, T., Frederickson, N. and Furnham, A. (2005) 'Explaining individual differences in scholastic behaviour and achievement'. *British Journal of Educational Psychology*, **75**, 239–55.

Piaget, J. (1977) The *Development of Thought: Equilibriation of Cognitive Structures*. New York: The Viking Press.

Platt, M. (2005) 'Primates may hold clues to autism and unfairness'. *The Psychologist*, **18**(4), 195.

Posner, M. (1996) 'Perception versus reality: school uniforms and the halo effect', in Miller, E., Graves-Desai, K. and Maloney, K. (eds) *The Harvard Education Letter*, **12**(1), 6.

Pusey, A. (1980) 'Inbreeding-avoidance in chimpanzees'. *Animal Behaviour*, **28**, 543–52.

Reid, B. (1993) ' "But we're doing it anyway": exploring a response to the concept of reflective practice in order to improve its facilitation'. *Nurse Education Today*, **13**, 305–9.

Rigby, K. (2004) 'Addressing bullying in schools: theoretical perspectives and their implications'. *School Psychology International*, **25**(3), 287–300.

Rivers, I. (2001) 'Bullying of sexual minorities at school: its nature and long-term correlates'. *Educational and Child Psychology*, **18**(1), 32–46.

Robertson, L. and Monsen, J. (2001) 'Issues in the development of a homosexual identity: practice implications for educational psychologists'. *Educational and Child Psychology*, **18**(1), 13–31.

Robson, C. (1993) *Real World Research*. Oxford: Blackwell.

Rogers, C.R. and Freiberg, H.J. (1994) *Freedom to Learn*. Columbus, OH: Merrill/Macmillan.

Rosenthal, R. and Jacobson, L. (1992) *Pygmalion in the Classroom – Teacher Expectation and Pupils' Intellectual Development*. Camarthen: Crown House Publishing.

Sackett, D., Rosenberg, W., Gray, J. and Richardson, W. (1996) 'Evidence based medicine: what it is and what it is not'. *British Medical Journal*, **312**, 71–2.

Sagar, H. and Schofield, J. (1980) 'Racial and behavioral cues in black and white children's perceptions of ambiguously aggressive'. *Journal of Personality and Social Psychology*, **39**(4), 590–8, October.

Schön, D. (1983) *The Reflective Practitioner*. New York: Basic Books.

Schön, D. (1987) *Educating the Reflective Practitioner*. San Francisco, CA: Jossey Bass.

Seagal, S. and Horne, D. (1985) *The Technology of Humanity*. Topanga Canyon: Human Dynamics.

Searle, C. (1997) *Living Community, Living School: Essays on Education in British Inner Cities*. London: Tufnell Press.

Selby-Bigge, L.A. (1924) *Psychological Tests of Educable Capacity*. London: HMSO.

Seligman (1975) *Helplessness: On Depression, Development, And Death*. San Francisco, CA: New York: W.H. Freeman.

Shaffer, H.R. (1984) *The Child's Entry into the Social World*. London, Academic Press.

Sherif, M. and Sherif, C. (1956) *An Outline of Social Psychology*. New York: Harper and Brothers.

Shi, J. and Zha, Z. (2000) 'Psychological research on the education of gifted and talented children in China', in *International Handbook of Gifted and Talented* (2nd edn) (ed. K. Heller). London: Pergamon.

Silver, H., Strong, R. and Perini, M. (1997) 'Integrating learning styles and multiple intelligences'. *Educational Leadership*, **55**(1), 22–7.

Skinner, B.F. (1957) *Verbal Behavior*. New York: Appleton.

Skinner, B.F. (1968) *The Technology of Teaching*. New York: Appleton.

Special Schools in Britain 2005–6. Bromsgrove: Ascent Publishing.

Spearman, C. (1904) 'General intelligence objectively determined and measured'. *American Journal of Psychology*, **5**, 201–93.

Sternberg, R. (1985) *Beyond IQ: A Triarchic Theory of Human Intelligence*. New York: Cambridge University Press.

Sternberg, R. (1999) 'A triarchic approach to the understanding and assessment of intelligence in multicultural populations'. *Journal of School Psychology*, **37**(2), 145–59.

Sternberg, R. and Grigorenko, E. (1997) 'The cognitive costs of physical and mental ill health: applying the psychology of the developed world to the problems of the developing world'. *Eye on Psi Chi*, **2**, 20–7.

Stevens, J., Quittner, A. and Abikoff, H. (1998) 'Factors influencing elementary school teachers' ratings of ADHD behaviour'. *Journal of Clinical Child Psychology*, **27**(4), 406–14.

Story, R. (1999) 'Inclusive education through effective teaching: increasing on-task time in secondary school classrooms'. Paper presented at Living at the Edge: International Conference on Young People and Social Exclusion. Strathclyde University, September 9–12.

Story, R. (2005) 'Interactive teaching and pupil engagement'. Personal communication. RstoryRick@aol.com.

Sweller, J. (1988) 'Cognitive load during problem solving: effects on learning'. *Cognitive Science*, **12**, 257–85.

Tajfel, H. and Wilkes, A. (1963) 'Classification and quantitative judgement', *British Journal of Psychology*, **54**, 101–14.

Terman, L.M. (1916) *The Uses of Intelligence Tests*. Boston, MA: Houghton Mifflin.

Thomas, L. and Harri-Augstein, S. (1985) *Self Organised Learning: Foundations of a Conversational Science for Psychology*. London: Routledge and Kegan Paul.

Thorndyke, E. (1920) 'A constant error in psychological ratings'. *Journal of Applied Psychology*, **4**, 25–9.

Thurstone, L.L. (1938) *Primary Mental Abilities*. Baltimore, MD: Williams and Wilkins.

Tuckman, B. and Jensen, M. (1977) 'Stages of small group development'. *Group and Organisational Studies*, **2**, 419–27.

Tyler, K. and Jones, B. (1998) 'Using the ecosystemic approach to change chronic problem behaviour in primary schools'. *Pastoral Care*, December, 11–20.

UNESCO (1994) *The Salamanca Statement and Framework for Action on Special Educational Needs*. Paris: UNESCO.

Van Geert, P. (1994) *Dynamic Systems of Development*. New York: Harvester.

VanTassel-Baska, J. (1998) *Gifted and Talented Learners*. Denver, CO: Love Publishing Company.

Vygotsky, L. (1929) 'The problem of the cultural development of the child'. *Journal of Genetic Psychology*, **36**, 415–32.

Vygotsky, L. (1978) *Mind in Society*. Cambridge, MA: Harvard University Press.

Walker, J. (1987) 'Comparison of specific patterns of antisocial behaviour in children with conduct disorder with or without coexisting hyperactivity'. *Journal of Consulting and Clinical Psychology*, **55**(6), 910–13.

Warren, R.M. (1970) 'Perceptual restoration of missing speech sounds'. *Science*, **167**(917), 392–3, January 23.

Wechsler, D. (1939) *The Measurement of Adult Intelligence*. Baltimore, MD: Williams and Wilkins.

Wechsler, D. (1992) *The Wechsler Intelligence Scale for Children* (3rd edn). (UK version). London: Psychological Corporation.

Wheldall, K. and Lam, Y.Y. (1987) 'Rows versus tables. II. The effects of two classroom seating arrangements on classroom disruption rate, on-task behaviour and teacher behaviour in three special school classes'. *Educational Psychology: An International Journal of Experimental Educational Psychology*, **7**(4), 303–12.

Wheldall, K., Houghton, S. and Merrett, K. (1989) 'Natural rates of teacher approval and disapproval in British secondary school classrooms'. *British Journal of Educational Psychology*, **59**, 38–48.

Wheldall, K., and Merrett, K. (1987) 'Natural rates of teacher approval and disapproval in British primary and middle school classrooms'. *British Journal of Educational Psychology*, **57**, 95–103.

Woolfson, R.C., Harker, M.E. and Lowe, D.A. (2004) 'Racism in schools – no room for complacency'. *Educational and Child Psychology*, **21**(4), 16–30.

Yerkes, R. (1918) 'Psychology in relation to the war'. *Psychological Review*, **25**, 85–115.

Index